SNATCHPROOF

The Art of Hearing God's Voice

I pray this book brings you closer to Him!

Wendy Selvig

WENDY SELVIG

WESTBOW PRESS
A DIVISION OF THOMAS NELSON
& ZONDERVAN

Copyright © 2014 Wendy Selvig.

All rights reserved. No part of this book may be used or reproduced by any means, graphic, electronic, or mechanical, including photocopying, recording, taping or by any information storage retrieval system without the written permission of the publisher except in the case of brief quotations embodied in critical articles and reviews.

WestBow Press books may be ordered through booksellers or by contacting:

WestBow Press
A Division of Thomas Nelson & Zondervan
1663 Liberty Drive
Bloomington, IN 47403
www.westbowpress.com
1 (866) 928-1240

Because of the dynamic nature of the Internet, any web addresses or links contained in this book may have changed since publication and may no longer be valid. The views expressed in this work are solely those of the author and do not necessarily reflect the views of the publisher, and the publisher hereby disclaims any responsibility for them.

Any people depicted in stock imagery provided by Thinkstock are models, and such images are being used for illustrative purposes only.
Certain stock imagery © Thinkstock.

ISBN: 978-1-4908-2979-1 (sc)
ISBN: 978-1-4908-2980-7 (e)

Library of Congress Control Number: 2014904820

Printed in the United States of America.

WestBow Press rev. date: 03/21/2014

This book is lovingly dedicated to

Erik,

Caleb,

and Josiah.

My three amazing sons!

This book is, and always was, written with you in mind. If I can teach you to hear the voice of the Lord in your life, I will have considered my not-so-perfect walk as your mother a success. I know He will walk with you throughout your lives. If you can hear God, I will not worry. If you hear Him, you'll be able to finish the race well. I love you boys so much!

Also, to my amazing husband and partner for life who let me bounce ideas off of him and who many times watched the kids while I snagged a few hours to write. Thank you Erik! I love you babe!

Last but not least, this book belongs to Him.
The One who leads us through this adventure we call
life. Thank you for making me Snatchproof Jesus!

Contents

Acknowledgements ix
Foreword xi

Chapter 1   Snatchproof 1
Chapter 2   Ways We Hear Him 7
Chapter 3   Hearing God in Your Thoughts 22
Chapter 4   Why God Speaks 30
Chapter 5   The Voice of An Enemy 40
Chapter 6   The Voice of God 49
Chapter 7   Hearing God Through Emotionally Charged and
            Tumultuous Times 59
Chapter 8   To Share or Not to Share, That is the Question 63
Chapter 9   Avoiding Flakiness! 66
Chapter 10 Exercises to Help You Hear God Speak 68
Chapter 11 Teaching Your Children To Hear God Speak 77
Chapter 12 A Higher Conscience 87
Chapter 13 Conclusion 92

ACKNOWLEDGEMENTS

Oral Granville Roberts was the first to speak into my life about hearing the voice of God. While attending Oral Roberts University I got to hear him speak in chapel and he was well known for challenging his students to learn to hear God's voice. In every class I attended I heard this theme and it was at this University that the idea of learning to hear God's voice took root. Many years later I had a vivid and impactful dream where Oral and many other great men and women of his generation of faith were sitting in the audience of a grand auditorium. They were watching to see what the next generation would do. I was preparing to go onto the stage and Oral handed me a baton and said to me, "It's your turn now, we've finished our race." I don't presume anything by that dream except that it truly is my generation's turn to teach the next one how to hear God's voice, and that is what I aim to do in this book.

Ted and Gayle Haggard are spiritual parents to my husband and I. We first heard Ted speak as college students at an ORU chapel service in the 1990's. After graduation we went to Colorado Springs to be a part of their church. If you know Ted's story, it is a true tale of grace and redemption that should give hope to any person who has ever fallen short of God's glory. I would not be where I am today without Pastor Ted and Gayle's influence and teaching.

Pastor Ted was the founding pastor of New Life Church (Colorado Springs, Colorado), and former president of the National Association of Evangelicals. Together Ted and Gayle grew New Life Church from a small group of people meeting in their home to a 14,000-member congregation.

In 2006, their world was rocked by scandal, and they stepped down from leadership to get healing and restoration. Since that time, Gayle and Ted have emerged from their crisis with their faith, marriage, and family stronger than ever because of what they experienced and learned. Today they lead Roundtable discussions with Christian leaders around the nation which focus on the idea of restoring the key ideas of the New Testament to the modern church's reputation. Ted and Gayle currently pastor St. James Church in Colorado Springs.

Thank you Pastor Ted and Gayle for showing me how to live life well and how to do things in a life giving way. That is your hallmark. Thank you!

Everett Daves is my father and is the most incredible editor and newspaper man I've ever known. Because of him I got to grow up with a dark room in our home, early typing lessons and the knowledge of learning how to write as a teenager. I couldn't have put this book together without his help and many hours of proof-reading! Thanks Dad!

FOREWORD

Once in a while we discover a person whose influence in our lives is nothing short of a gift from heaven. Wendy Selvig has proven to be such a person to me. From the time I first met her, she has spoken words of insight, affirmation and encouragement to me that have resonated in the deeper places of my spirit. According to her, she can't help it. God's Spirit speaks to her and she knows when He does.

In her book, *Snatchproof,* Wendy shares with us what she has learned about hearing God's voice. Within its pages she reveals her refined wisdom as she shows us not only how to hear, but also how to respond wisely and lovingly to the thoughts and inspirations of God's Spirit within us.

I have observed Wendy as she quietly carries out what she professes. She does so in a most appealing, practical, and non-judgmental way. I am inspired by her life lived out in sincere faith and ministry as I have been among many who have been well-served and deeply blessed by it. As you read this book, you will be too.

-Gayle Haggard, is the author of the New York Times best-selling book**, *Why I Stayed: the Choices I Made in my Darkest Hour,*** and her newest book**, *Courageous Grace.*** She is an author, speaker, and wife of Ted Haggard.

Chapter 1

Snatchproof

> "My sheep listen to my voice; I know them, and they follow me. I give them eternal life, and they shall never perish; <u>no one will snatch them out of my hand.</u>"
> – John 10:27

God Speaks

Is God real? If He is, does He speak to people? If so, how does He do it and why is it so hard for people to figure it out?

When I discovered the answers to these questions, my world changed forever. Until I went to college, I don't remember ever being taught to hear God's voice. And then when I tried the principles I learned and actually heard Him speak with clarity, it changed my life forever.

I went to Oral Roberts University in the 1990's while Oral Roberts was still alive. Rev. Roberts was a world-wide famous and sometimes controversial Pentecostal televangelist and healer dating back to the 1950's and 1960's. He was the chancellor of the university when I attended and he was in his final years. I feel privileged to have heard him speak several times.

Rev. Roberts told his students that if they only learned one thing in life, it needed to be how to hear God's voice. He said that if you learned this one skill, you'd be successful in whatever field you studied, because the Spirit of God would be able to guide you towards success and away from the pitfalls. I took him for his word and the desire to learn to hear God's voice was stirred within me.

I learned a few basic methods of hearing God's voice from Rev. Robert's teaching, and as I began to hear God more clearly, I learned more from the Holy Spirit Himself. In this book, I'm going to offer you the principles I use to hear God speaking in my own life. My hope is to help you to hear Him too.

Before we dive into how to hear His voice, let's get a little perspective as to *why* we need to hear Him. Let's look at a few scriptures that give us the big picture on what is really going on in this life.

1 Corinthians 13:12 – "For now we see only a reflection as in a mirror; then we shall see face to face. Now I know in part; then I shall know fully, even as I am fully known."
My quick two cents: In our current existence, we are blinded to full truth and it is difficult to see the big picture -what is really going on.

2 Corinthians 5:7 – "For we live by faith, not by sight."
My quick two cents: Because we are blinded to the full truth, we must learn to trust that God knows more and sees better than we do. This takes learning to trust that He has our best interests at heart.

Romans 8:23-24 – "Not only so, but we ourselves, who have the first fruits of the Spirit, groan inwardly as we wait eagerly for our adoption to sonship, the redemption of our bodies."
My quick two cents: Our bodies apparently need to be redeemed. I think the curse that came on mankind affected our bodies. When He returns, scripture suggests our bodies will be like His (and like they were supposed to be from the beginning): incorruptible, powerful, spiritual, physical, eternal, not broken, beautiful and glorious. (See: 1 Cor.: 42-22, 15:52-52, 15:35-38, 2 Co 5:1-5, Is 35:3-5, Col:9-11, Zech. 9:16-17, Mal 3:16-17, Ps 17:15).

Romans 8:20-21 – "For the creation was subjected to frustration, not by its own choice, but by the will of the one who subjected it, in hope that the creation itself will be liberated from its bondage to decay and brought into the freedom and glory of the children of God."

My quick two cents: All of creation suffered under the Fall. When God's glory returns to the earth, everything in creation will be restored.

Luke 12:7a – "Indeed, the very hairs of your head are all numbered."
My quick two cents: This means someone is keeping track!

Revelation 20:12- "And I saw the dead, great and small, standing before the throne, and books were opened. Another book was opened, which is the book of life. The dead were judged according to what they had done as recorded in the books."
My quick two cents: This is a heavy scripture but it does show that the details of our life are being recorded. Again, someone is keeping track.

1 Corinthians 9:24 –25 "Do you not know that in a race all the runners run, but only one gets the prize? Run in such a way as to get the prize. Everyone who competes in the games goes into strict training. They do it to get a crown that will not last, but we do it to get a crown that will last forever."
My quick two cents: There is *purpose* to life and at the end there is a prize or reward of some kind. We need to learn how to run this race well so that we win the prize. We don't want to run aimlessly and fail the test!

Are you starting to get the idea that there is something going on behind the scenes that we don't always see? According to these Scriptures, we don't yet see the whole picture clearly. We are in essence, walking blindly. Yet we need to find a way to win this test of life victoriously.

There is a way designed by God to help us win. It's the way He has intended us to walk since the beginning. It was the way laid out in the Garden of Eden and is shown with the idea of a walk with God in the cool of the morning. It's through relationship and mentorship from God Himself. It's what He's always wanted with you and me. It is, in my view, *the big lesson* we are supposed to learn in life.

What better way to win a race then to have a personal trainer? We need someone who knows the rules, knows the track, and knows how to navigate and train us so that we can run the race and win!

Jesus is supposed to be our personal trainer! God designed it this way. He sent His son and stated that no man will come to the Father except through Jesus. His is the only voice that can lead and guide you through the pitfalls of life. He is the One who wants to help you win the race. He's rooting for you and cheering you on!

Life is too complicated to live without hearing His voice. Pitfalls await us. Sin entangles us. Fear controls us. Doubt destroys us. We walk around blindly, trying to make it on our own and somehow think we can stumble our way to a victorious end. It just doesn't happen that way.

Hindrances like sin, fear and doubt are purposely laid out for us by an enemy we can't see. John 10:10 says that "The thief's purpose is to steal and kill and destroy." If the enemy gets you to turn away from and reject the Shepherd, he is able to snatch you out of God's hands. That is his ultimate goal. His war is against God and you are to be the casualty.

Because the war takes place in a realm you cannot physically see, and takes place mostly in your mind, this enemy is able to cause offense and harm you without being noticed. He's able to hide behind thoughts you think are your own. He can manipulate you and cause you to stumble. That is, until you know that the enemy is there and what his voice sounds like. (I promise to show you!)

In John 10: 27-28, Jesus says "My sheep listen to my voice; I know them, and they follow me. I give them eternal life, and they will never perish. No one can snatch them away from me." The key to being Snatchproof is to be able to hear God's voice. You then can avoid all of the pitfalls because He guides you gently away from them.

So with that in mind, you're about to hear a very one-sided argument. I believe strongly in the idea of an immanent God, meaning that God is present and deals intimately with individuals as they live their lives. I'm 100% convinced, without a shadow of a doubt, that God is real, in love with you, and wanting to communicate with you on a daily basis. I want to show you what His character is like and who He is, so that you have a good chance in life to walk victoriously, knowing who you are: a loved child of God.

I also want to show you how to avoid appearing to be one of the *crazies* who say they hear something from God but truly do not. I hope to show you how to know if it is God speaking and whether you should mention it to anyone else or keep God's Word quietly to yourself.

In scripture, Jesus says that "My sheep hear my voice and they know me." Jesus promises that if you put your trust in Him, you will have eternal life. It's as simple as saying to God in prayer, "I accept your gift. I will trust in You." When you accept that gift, you are beginning on a journey of learning who Jesus is, and what He promises for you. His gift redeems you from your broken state of separation from Him. He seals you with His Spirit, and He promises to counsel you. Jesus said that if you belong to Him, you will hear His voice. This book is designed to help you see what that really means.

God loves you. He wants to be involved in your life. He has a purpose and a plan for your life if you'll only have faith to receive it. What proof do I have for this statement? As we say at our church, "I am the living proof!" In fact, I do have a relationship with Jesus. He is closer than a brother. He speaks to me. He is involved in the details. He tells me things that I could not know on my own. He has warned me of dangers. He has spoken to me in the quiet.

Hearing His voice has allowed me to go deeper spiritually than I ever thought possible. When darkness seemed to surround me, He spoke loving things to me like, "My sweet daughter, I love you. I will not forsake you. Trust me and see the crooked paths be made straight." When I was looking for direction at a vocational fork in the road, He told me which path was the best. When my husband and I were trying to decide to buy a house, He spoke to me and told me that yes, we should "go forward" and our house would be a place of peace and the Spirit of God would be present there. When I faced a period of infertility, He spoke to me words of comfort and faith saying, "I know exactly who your children are going to be and when they will join your family. Do not fear." At times when life has been overwhelming and I find myself seeking God for comfort, I've heard Him whisper things that led me to peace and assurance. He's truly a Shepherd that leads us by still waters. He truly strengthens and comforts and leads us if we will let Him.

There have been times when God has spoken to me and told me deep details about another person that I couldn't know on my own. Those times serve a purpose and I will share some of those stories within these pages.

Truly hearing His voice is more than imagination or wishful thinking. And, what's truly special about it is that I consider myself just a regular person. If I can learn to hear Him, you can learn to hear Him too!

He wants this kind of relationship with you. He wants to gently lead and guide you through the rough patches of life so that you do not stumble. He wants to lead you beside still waters and help you find places to rest when life seems weary. He wants you to be able to hear His voice so you feel the assurance in your heart that He is real and that He sees you and knows you. And, He wants you to be Snatchproof! How do I know this is so? Let me show you!

Chapter 2

Ways We Hear Him

"My sheep hear my voice and I know them." –John 10:27

God is a communicator. He's a creator and an artist. He can express Himself in many ways. The question is not so much of how He speaks, but really it is in what ways can we hear Him?

I find it interesting how different personality types seem to hear Him in different ways. An artistic person may hear Him well through symbols and visions while someone who values order and organization may hear Him more through the reading of His Word.

Your personality may influence the natural ways you are bent towards hearing Him, and what ways you are open to hearing Him speak.

He Speaks Through His Word

God gave us the Bible, His inspired Word, specifically to lead us and guide us through this life. No matter our bent, we must learn to know Him through His Word. Hebrews 4:12 tells us that the Word of God is alive and active. It's sharper than any double-edged sword. It penetrates even to dividing soul and spirit, joints and marrow; it judges the thoughts and attitudes of the heart. God has spoken throughout the ages to many authors who wrote down what He told them to write and yet it seems as if there was only one writer. This collection of books spans thousands of years yet remains relevant today.

As I've learned to hear God speak to me through ways other than the Bible, I found it was necessary to compare the new experiences to the Word of God. As Hebrews says, it judges the thoughts and attitudes of the heart. When you're trying to decide if God is speaking, you compare the experience with His Word and if it doesn't agree it's not from Him.

God promises the heavens and the earth will pass away but His Word will not. That means He isn't going to change His mind about what He has said and He isn't going to give us new information outside of His Word that changes anything already written there. Anyone who claims to add to God's Word or takes away from it is in eternal danger. This is mentioned in the last book of the Bible, Revelation. Don't be tempted to think God would tell you a new revelation that doesn't line up with Scripture. If you think that, I can guarantee it's not God's voice you are hearing.

As you read the Bible, there are times when God will speak to you through it. Have you ever read something and felt as though the words popped off the page into your heart? This is the Holy Spirit illuminating the Word to you. He is lighting up a passage to speak to you about it. You will know this happens when what you have read becomes personal.

When a passage jumps off the page and appeals to you on an emotional level, it is my experience that the Holy Spirit is engaging you and trying to communicate with you.

The Bible is such a unique book. It was written by over 40 different people from many walks of life. Kings and fishermen, poets and peasants all had a hand in writing it. It was written in different places, at different times, and in many different moods. It was even written on different continents and in different languages. Still, behind the voices of the men who wrote the individual books, is the one Voice of the God who inspired the words. He trumpets His existence for the world to hear by using many men in many circumstances to create one book that reads as if it has one Author – and that is exactly what it has. Instead of choosing just one person to give an inspired book to, He showed that it did not matter who the writer was, He was still able to give us a book supernaturally through many different writers. There is a reason the Bible is the number one selling book of all time!

He Speaks Through Peace and Unrest

"For to us a child is born, to us a son is given, and the government will be on his shoulders. And he will be called Wonderful Counselor, Mighty God, Everlasting Father, *Prince of Peace*." - Isaiah 9:6 (Italics mine.)

When I ask people how God leads or speaks to them, one of the common responses I hear is that they go by the peace they feel in their hearts.

God's voice brings peace. Psalm 85:8 says, "I will hear what God the LORD will speak: for he will speak peace unto his people, and to his saints: but let them not turn again to folly."

Whenever you hear a *voice* or have a thought that brings fear, anxiety, trepidation, it's generally safe to say that it's not from God. However, that's not to say God cannot warn you if you are walking down a path that is putting you in danger. If you believe in Jesus and trust in Him, The Holy Spirit is within you. If you are headed down the wrong road, He works to trouble you about the path you are on. Likewise, if you are asking for direction and you feel no resistance in your heart, but instead you feel very peaceful about it, then the Holy Spirit is letting you proceed.

I have learned that when I have peace in my heart towards something, God is in agreement. When He is trying to steer me in another direction, I don't feel peace about whatever I am seeking Him on.

In my early college years, I dated one young man off and on for several years. He was attractive, had a good heart and was someone who was seeking God's will for his life. I liked him a lot and I wanted it to work out between us. But whenever I prayed about it I had no peace. He didn't feel peace either. He told me once that he felt like he was sitting next to another man's wife! No matter how hard I tried to ignore the feeling of unrest, it never would go away. I can only assume that I was wrong for this young man and he wrong for me. We had both submitted our search for the right person to our Shepherd and He was leading us through the lack of peace in our hearts.

When I began dating my husband Erik, not only did I fall head over heels for him, for the first time in my life I had absolute peace about the relationship. It was such a strange feeling because I had never experienced it before in regards to dating men. I was shocked by the peace I felt when I was with him.

Another example of this is when I worked for a ministry. I was tempted to look for another job because the ministry position I was holding didn't pay very much money. I would pray about leaving the job and not feel peaceful about it. When I would think about staying where I was, I just felt better. There was no unrest. I knew for that certain time, God was leading me to stay where I was. I could tell by the peace in my heart what I was supposed to do.

Larry Williamson, a pastor I know from a church in St. Louis, MO. writes about a time where the peace of God probably saved his life:

"When I was the lead evangelist for our church, we would take our street ministry team into the inner city of St Louis. We met on Saturday nights and the team would gather and pray first before going out. While we were praying one Saturday I kept feeling the urge to stay in and just pray. When I told the team we were going to just pray I felt great peace.

Three days later I found out that right where we were going to set up our outdoor ministry, four people had been shot and killed the very night and place we were going to go. We knew then that God had kept us in for our protection. If it were not for His voice of peace leading us, we would have been there. I always thank God for his voice speaking to me."

Another friend from college wrote about her decision to marry her husband Steve. Sarah writes: "I had graduated from college with a degree in missions and Steve and I had been really close friends for nine years. We both loved the Lord, and had started to look at each other as more than friends, but I didn't want to fall for a guy who didn't have a heart for missions. He had just completed his Master's degree in Engineering.

"I was headed to India for two months, and we decided that we'd pray about it over the time I was gone.

"While I was in India, Steve went to one of the mothers in the faith that we both knew, and told her that he felt he was falling in love with me, and that God had been stirring his heart toward missions over the last few months but that he was afraid to tell me, for fear that I would think that he was trying to manipulate the situation.

"What's funny is that I had gone to the same sweet mother in the faith, and told her that I was falling in love with Steve but my hesitation was that he didn't have a heart for missions. So, off I went to India asking God to show me. But all I felt, the whole two months, was just a peace, that even though it didn't make sense to my mind, it made sense in my spirit that God had brought us together and that he would work out the details and use us together to accomplish His will.

"So, I get home from India, and Steve proceeds to tell me that the Lord had in fact been stirring his heart toward missions for a while, and that he thought we should pursue a relationship and plan for marriage. Steve was shocked when I just agreed and said, "OK."

"We were engaged three months later and were married nine months after that. And, here we sit thirteen years later, having served overseas for a year, taken a number of short term trips, worked with missions agencies, and are still actively living and pursuing God's call and involvement for us in missions."

He Speaks Through Other People

One of the ways God speaks is through other people. He can use other people to speak to you directly with a prophetic word or He can use them indirectly without them knowing it.

I have had times where someone has approached me and said, "The Lord wants you to know…" and they proceed to give me the message. That undoubtedly gets my attention as it would anyone, but those times are not the normal nor the usual way that God speaks to me through people.

Often when I am praying and needing an answer, God uses people to bring the answers without them even knowing He's using them. For example, if I am praying about a health issue for one of my children and then that week I hear a friend talk about a supplement that addresses that specific issue, the friend has no idea I've been asking for that answer and yet God has brought them across my path.

When I was pregnant with our second son Caleb, Erik and I had a hard time picking out a name for him. Every name I came up with my husband strongly disliked. This went on for six to seven months of the pregnancy.

I prayed and asked God to name our child. I asked Him to pick out a name that would be a blessing to the child and that would be the right name for him. I knew that God knew my son already and He understood his future. God would have the right name. When I asked Him, I heard a still quiet voice in my mind (a thought) say, "Caleb."

I thought, "Was that really you Lord? Did you say Caleb?" And I was pretty sure that I had heard Him. But this was a name. This was something that would affect this child for the rest of his life. I had to absolutely know without a shadow of a doubt that God had said this.

So I asked Him for two confirmations. The first test would be that when I told Erik the name, he had to absolutely love it. I wanted no "that might work" comments. It had to be a passionate response from him. Second, and this was the true test, I wanted someone to out of the blue suggest the name to me. This was my specific litmus test.

"Lord, let someone just randomly suggest this name."

Now some will say I shouldn't have put God to the test like this, but I was so desperate to know if this was God's work or not. And I don't know if it was right to ask God to answer this way, but I had faith that He would, and He did.

That night I hesitantly said to Erik, "What about the name Caleb?" I will never forget the look on his face. He cocked his head a little and thought about it. Then, with a smile he said, "I love it!"

"Really?" Remember, this man had not liked a single name I had suggested in seven months.

With a smile from ear to ear he said, "Yes, I really love it! That's it! That's the name!" My faith began to rise as the first of my tests were answered by God.

So then, the very next day a sister-in-law called to chat. She wasn't married, didn't have children and the proceeding conversation seemed out of the ordinary to me. Right out of the blue she says, "If I were having a baby right now, I would call him Caleb. It's my favorite boy name."

I was absolutely amazed! God did exactly the two things I had requested to know for certain He had spoken. And, He did it with style. If I had had that conversation with my sister-in-law a month later, it wouldn't have had the same effect as it did being the very next day after my prayer. God used my sister-in-law to confirm something He had spoken and she wasn't even aware of it.

That is my experience with God using other people. They often don't know that what they have said means something to you, but yet it does and it's personal and it's between you and God. He's like that. He's personal. He loves you, sees you, and communicates on a personal level.

He Speaks Through Circumstances, Serendipitous Moments, and Recognizable Patterns.

If you're scientific-minded, this method of hearing God may be easier for you to understand than others. This method has actually been given a name by scientists. It's called Design Inference and is used to recognize intelligent patterns in nature where there shouldn't be any.

The idea of Design Inference, in layman's terms, is that we can distinguish between events that are caused by intelligence and undirected natural causes. Design Inference reveals intelligent causes (i.e. God) by recognizing specified events of small probability. Just about anything that happens is highly improbable, but when a highly improbable event is also specified (conforms to a pattern), undirected natural causes lose their explanatory power. In other words, we can see God work when He uses something ordinary in our lives and creates an unordinary pattern out of it.

An example is Mount Rushmore. You can look at any of the hills of South Dakota and see weathered patterns carved into the rock, but when you look at Mount Rushmore, you see designs that match a recognizable pattern. You recognize the faces of the four famous presidents and know those faces are there by design, not by chance. When we look at Mount Rushmore, we see an indication of intelligence that is not put there by the wind, rain, and elements. The sculpture of the recognizable faces indicates intelligence.

I'd like to apply this same Design Inference to the idea of hearing from God. When things start jumping out at you in your life and you start to recognize a pattern in what would normally be random life happenings, it is an indication that God wants you to notice something is different. It's then that you ask yourself, "What is God trying to speak to me about?"

Which reminds me of a very personal experience I had with God involving owls. I may risk sounding a little crazy by telling you this, but it's a perfect example of how the Lord can speak through patterns.

First of all, before this *owl* day, I had never noticed owls. Other than Winnie the Pooh or Snow White in a scary forest, who does? They seem smart, usually show up at night, and their call sounds like they only want to know who's there. But in my day-to-day life, I just don't encounter them very often.

It all started when my son came home from school and handed me a sculpted owl.

"Did you make this at school, honey?"

"Yep," he said, all smiles.

"Thank you so much! You did an awesome job." I put it on my desk, proudly displaying his artwork.

That afternoon, as I was trying to help my younger son find his favorite cartoon, I saw a trailer for "Legend of the Guardians: The Owls of Ga'Hoole."

No big deal and kind of random, but my brain made a connection. I didn't think much of it.

Then, as I was going through my daily email, I came across a greeting card from a friend. This, too, had an owl as part of the image. All three occurrences were random and I still wasn't thinking that God was speaking to me but my brain did pick up on the pattern of owls showing up in my day.

But all of this was nothing compared to what happened later that night. As I turned out the lights and got into bed, I heard a strange sound coming from outside my window. As my brain processed this sound and realized what it was, I did a double take and looked to the window to see an owl, sitting on my roof right under my window, staring and hooting at me like he's trying to get me a message.

Here was an undeniable pattern with a dramatic ending. God wanted to tell me something.

Even though I can't prove anything except circumstantial evidence, I am aware that something was different and it concerned owls. This may sound crazy to someone who has never experienced God speaking this way, but it is this pattern that caused me to take notice.

In this situation I called my brother who I like to talk with about these kinds of things. My brother was a pastor for over 20 years and is very sensitive to hearing the Lord speak to him.

He said, "That's neat that you're seeing owls. Lots of people I know who walk in the prophetic are seeing owls lately. As a matter of fact, I was just at a conference where there was a big discussion on it and what it means. There is talk that God is speaking to us about owls because owls are called the eagle of the night. Owls can see clearly in the dark and America seems to be plunging into darkness right now. If you are seeing owls, you can see in the darkness and you can demolish your prey with no trouble. As a matter of fact, the owl's favorite meal is serpent."

I love the idea of destroying the work of the enemy! I had been praying about some things and asking God about writing this book with the purpose of helping people see in the dark by learning to hear His voice. His answer was so distinctively Him, full of creativity and it had a wow factor that helped me know it really was from Him. It was a confirmation to me that I should go ahead and write this book!

Because I know God speaks this way, I've learned to sit up and take notice whenever a pattern emerges where there shouldn't be one. When this type of thing happens to you, ask Him to reveal the message or whatever He is trying to speak to you about. Usually within a day or two, I have my answer, and I've learned something amazing from God. Again I am reminded about how involved He is in the details of my life and how magnificent He is.

Here is a hypothetical example of how God may speak to you in this way. Maybe you are wondering If you should find a new job. You ask God for wisdom and direction and to help you know if you should change your vocation. Then over the course of the next week the following things start to happen:

Every time you turn on the radio you hear a commercial for an online job search service. Then, a friend asks you out of the blue if you are going to be staying with your current job or not. You hear a song on the radio that has the line in it, "Get a job." Your mother calls and asks if you've ever considered another vocation. Your boss lets you know that over the next year they will be downsizing.

All of these things on their own mean little, but when they start accumulating, you start to take notice. Now sometimes these things could be coincidences, but if you are aware of the pattern developing, He might be getting your attention. It might be time to pray about it and ask Him to reveal what He's showing you, if He's showing you something.

My dear friend Cha (pronounced "Shay"), who was a chaplain friend of mine in college, wrote to me about how she hears God through these patterns of life and she calls them "serendipitous moments."

"I've been thinking a lot about how I hear God and if I hear Him at all. What I know is that I have experiences daily that I need to talk to God about and want to hear what to do, or what next step to take. I have yet to hear an audible voice tell me what street to stroll down, corner to turn or path to take. But strange things happen as I take the next step that seems before me; serendipitous things start to occur.

"I see the billboard, while driving home from work that leads me to that very thing I have been praying about. Or, I meet that person that introduces me to a supplement that addresses a health issue I've been putting before God for some time.

In the ether of life, as I walk, pray and talk with God . . . as I try to be everything He dreamt and everything He wants me to be, I see Him unfolding His voice in the motion of my days. You see, with great finesse God speaks to me in the magical movement of life. I used to get mad that I didn't hear Him. I used to pray and try to invoke the God of the Old Testament that speaks to people in a voice of thunder on mountain tops. I use to do all of this until I realized that I SAW His voice. My life mirrors conversations I have with God. He makes my life look like what we chat about all the time. . . yes indeed, the serendipitous voice of God. "

He Speaks Through Symbols

"Great is our Lord and mighty in power; His understanding has no limit." (Psalms 147:5)

God uses symbols all throughout the Bible. I would say that symbols are no stranger to the language of God. Just try to read Revelation without considering symbols and you'd be in a world of hurt. I don't know many people who have heard God speak through symbols, but I do know some.

I do believe this is a viable way He speaks. He is an intimate friend who knows us so well that He can use a symbol as an inside message or communication. The key to understanding this method of communication from God is first of all recognizing it is possible. If you recognize it and are open to it, He may choose to speak to you knowing you'll receive it.

My brother Daniel is a creative person. He's a musician, marketer, and artist. One of the ways God gets his attention is through the symbol of an eagle. It's like he and God have a little inside understanding. Whenever eagles start appearing, he snaps to attention because he realizes God is trying to get him to see something.

When Daniel is seeking direction, the Lord has eagles appear in his life. I wouldn't believe it if I hadn't seen it myself. Sometimes real ones appear, other times he's gotten an eagle sculpture delivered unexpectedly from a friend or a card in the mail with an eagle on it. They just keep appearing when he's looking for confirmation from the Lord.

One time he wanted to buy a house. He had looked at many places and wondered which one was the right one. He went to the house he thought might be it and as he was praying, a bald eagle came and landed on the telephone wire outside the house. This was in the middle of a large city. Not a common place for eagles to hang out. It meant something to him, but for a person not looking for symbols, it wouldn't mean a thing.

Another friend, Floyd, had this story to share:

"Sometimes He speaks to me in simple things. A few months ago, my relationship with my girlfriend was just beginning. It was a Saturday, and my son and I were going to church. As I was getting on the highway, I look back to merge into traffic and I saw her in her car driving towards me. I was struck by the symbolism of it. It was like God was saying He was bringing us together."

Why wouldn't God use symbolism to speak to someone? He did it in the Bible all the time. Also, think of a person who is an artist, who thinks in symbols, who recognizes coincidences for more than circumstance. God made that person, and God knows his or her language. He knows how to communicate with that person in the best way and He is not too straight-laced to do it. God is wild and passionate and in love with you. He'll reach out to you to communicate however He can. Some denominations will declare that the Bible is the only communication God has given us, and they justify that by saying "it is enough." They think you shouldn't need to hear God speaking in any other way.

Yet I would challenge this way of thinking. First of all, there is no scripture that indicates that God does not speak to us outside of the Bible. On the contrary, He has filled us with the Holy Spirit. He is a living being who leads and guides us. Yes, He guides us through His Word. Absolutely. And, I've already said you must compare every word and thought to the Scripture to make certain it is true.

But are we limited to the book only?

God has historically worked in different ways with different people. According to 1 Corinthians 12:11 the Holy Spirit gives different abilities to different people. He obviously works with us in different ways!

Now many people who aren't creative, aren't artists, and don't appreciate symbols might never look for a symbol from the Lord. And if they saw an eagle when praying about something, they would never make the connection that the Lord, the grand artist of all artists, might speak to a person that way. So maybe the Lord wouldn't bother speaking to that person through a symbol. That's not a slam on that person; it's just saying that God will speak to one person differently than another. It's not favoritism on God's part, it's just that I think He chooses to speak to you the way you'll receive it the best. So, your job is to figure out the best way you can hear or accept Him speaking to you, and then look for Him to do it.

He Speaks Through Visions

"In the last days, God says, I will pour out my Spirit on all people. Your sons and daughters will prophesy, your young men will see visions, your old men will dream dreams." – Acts 2:17

Another way God speaks is through visions. This could be a sensitive topic for some people because some denominations believe that God no longer speaks in this way. I have friends who believe that these kinds of things died out with the last apostles. I have heard the argument but for the person who has had a vision, and I say this in love, the argument flies out the window.

A vision is a hard thing to describe to someone who has never had one. I believe there are different levels of visions from a full out *open vision* where you are there in the middle of an experience to the more common *mind's eye type* of vision.

A Picture is Worth a Thousand Words

The best way I know how to describe the *mind's eye* type of a vision is that it is like a memory. Think for a moment of a Christmas morning from your childhood. Do you remember the picture window where your parents always set up the Christmas tree? Or maybe it was in the corner by the fireplace. What about what you were wearing? New footie pajamas or a favorite sweater with fluffy slippers? What did the furniture look like? Comfy and cool or old and tattered? And the scents! Can you smell the ham in the oven, or the pine scent filling the air from a freshly cut tree? These are all details that you don't have to work hard to remember. They are just there when you bring up the memory. You can close your eyes and look around to see the details of the room.

In my mother's house while I was growing up, we had a shag brown sofa (this was the 1980's) that was the softest thing you ever sat on. I can imagine the feel and the smell of that sofa in an instant when remembering.

A vision to many people is like a memory. You don't have to work to create the details; they are just there in your mind's eye. It's like looking around a memory, only it isn't a memory, it's all new information. It's something God wants to communicate to you personally.

The first time I remember having a vision was on a missions trip to Uganda, Africa. I was there with a group from my university for two months. We traveled to many villages and cities and held meetings. We preached the good news of salvation through Jesus. We saw many miracles happen.

Several hours before one of the tent meetings I was praying and I saw a vivid and clear picture in my mind's eye of an African woman. She was looking through a photo album and all of the pictures were black and white. As she turned the pages they began to turn into color photos. I believed the Lord was showing me that there would be a color-blind woman who would be healed that night.

Later, when the service was about over, we held an altar call. I stepped up to the microphone and invited people to come forward who needed to be healed in their body. I then asked if there was anyone who was color-blind. One of the ladies at the altar raised her hand. We prayed for her and she was healed instantly. She jumped up and down in excitement as she exclaimed to the crowd that she was seeing new colors. She could see color for the first time!

Our team leader later told me he thought I was crazy when I had asked if anyone was color-blind. This true vision from God helped us minister effectively. And, I was glad to know I hadn't gone off the deep end!

Now **open visions** are a little different. An aunt of mine experienced an open vision. This is her story:

"We had a visitor at our church who was running for a local office. She was sitting a few rows in front of me and I kept seeing a flicker that would cause me to look at her back. She got up during part of the service and went up front to have the pastor pray for her.

When she stood up, I saw him. A giant angel hovered above and behind her. His huge wings spread out to protect her. As the pastor prayed over her, the angel glanced my way. His eyes seared into me as he engulfed her in his wings. I could feel the protection he offered her.

Weeks later, the election was over and she hadn't won. In my mind, I knew God had answered her prayer – maybe not in the way she wanted but in a way that protected her from harm."

I asked my aunt about this vision to clarify which type of vision it was. She replied, "The angel was physically there as far as I was concerned. I felt like I could get up and touch him. He looked at me once and I felt such peace. I know the difference of the visions you are talking about. The angel was real, where other times I see a vision in my mind's eye. He was solid and big and a real presence. How I wish I could see that angel again!"

He Speaks Through Dreams

Leo was a seventeen-year-old boy from China who stayed with our family for three years while attending high school in the United States as a foreign exchange student. When he came to live with us he was a professing Buddhist.

Though Christians, we made it clear to Leo he did not need to be a Christian to live with us. He chose to go to a Christian high school on his own before we met him, because he recognized a spiritual void in his culture. In China there are tight restraints on organized religion. When I took him to enroll at his high school, he asked if he was required to be a

Christian to go there. I told him absolutely not, that he was free to believe what he wanted in the United States. He was visibly relieved to hear that.

Before Christmas, Leo was working on a paper for one of his classes. In it he had to describe his religion and what he believed. As I was helping him with the paper, he said, "I do not believe in Buddha and I don't believe in Jesus. I only believe in myself." He explained that he has prayed to Buddha before and Buddha has never helped him. I suggested he try doing that with Jesus sometime. He told me, "If Jesus is real, He can speak to me in a dream. If He comes to me in a dream, I will know He is real. Until then, I will just believe in myself." I nodded in agreement and thanked God for this kid who truly needed to hear from God.

In December, we bought a live Christmas tree at the local corner lot. The day after we brought it home it started losing needles. The tree was in serious trouble the week before Christmas. Late one night, in a last minute decision, my husband decided to drive up to the forest and cut down a fresh tree. Knowing Leo had already gone to bed, I shot him an email and told him that my husband Erik was going to cut down a tree in the morning, if he wanted to go. Well, little did I know that God would use that to speak to Leo.

The next morning Leo came bounding up the stairs saying, "I believe! I believe Jesus!" He was so excited!

He said, "I had a dream last night where Jesus spoke to me. " He apparently spoke some personal things to Leo. Then, "He told me that when I woke up in the morning, to prove the dream was real, we'd be going to get a Christmas tree!"

When Leo woke up from the dream, he saw my email for the first time. God had spoken to him in a dream and then confirmed it by telling him something he did not know. How cool is that?! God spoke to Leo in a dream to introduce Himself to him!

He Speaks Through Our Thoughts

Hearing God in our thoughts is so much of a game changer, I have written the entire next chapter on it. To walk through life knowing how to hear Him in our minds is a powerful thing indeed but I think it's typically the most difficult to master. We'll cover that in the next chapter.

Chapter 3

Hearing God in Your Thoughts

"My sheep hear my voice and I know them,
and they follow me." - John 10:27

Hearing God's Voice In Your Thoughts

"She has a secret struggle with pornography and an unhealthy Internet chat room relationship." That was one of the first things the Lord shared with me about another person when I was learning to hear His voice.

I was a senior at Oral Roberts University, and I was the chaplain for an entire dorm floor of girls. I had heard many preachers and chapel speakers talk about how they had heard the Lord lead, guide or speak to them. I was so hungry to know what it was like to hear God speak. There were times I had thought God had maybe spoken to me or had led me, but I wasn't sure. Was I supposed to hear an audible voice or would it be a thought in my head? I didn't know.

Being a chaplain, I was charged with the spiritual lives of 20 girls. I would often walk the hall at night laying my hands on their doors to pray for them. That year I asked God to show me how to hear His voice. I would journal while praying for the girls, writing down any thought or impression I felt while praying for them.

The first time I remember hearing Him speak (though I didn't know it at the time), I was praying specifically for one of the girls on my floor. For her protection, I'll change her name and call her *Lacey*. I laid my hands on her door and began to pray for her. A thought came into my head:

"She has a secret struggle with pornography and an unhealthy Internet chat room relationship." I didn't hear it audibly, it was just a thought. It wasn't judgmental in tone; it was just a fact that popped into my mind. I remember thinking, "That couldn't be God, that was my own thought. Shame on me for thinking that about her." I prayed for her but didn't mention it to anyone, convinced that I must have made it up in my head.

Well, one day a few weeks later Lacey knocked on the door of my dorm room needing someone to talk to. She poured her broken heart out to me admitting that she had a struggle with pornography and that she had recently begun a relationship with an older man in an Internet chat room. My jaw almost hit the floor, but not from the shock of what she was admitting. It was the shock of realization that I had actually heard God's voice and that it came in the form of a thought. I also realized that He had told me that about her so that I could help her and pray for and with her. He had compassion on his daughter and he had entrusted me with private information so that I could understand her struggle and be there for her.

So, I had heard him! I had finally heard God speak. Like I said before, it wasn't audible, it was a thought. Yet it wasn't a thought that originated with me.

So, this caused other questions to surface. If God spoke the thought to my mind, how many times had He spoken to me before? Without knowing He speaks to me through thoughts, I would likely have thought His voice was my own. And I do believe in the devil and demons, so does that mean that demons could speak to me as well and make me think they were my own thoughts? These questions began to bubble up as I was just at the beginning of my journey to hearing the voice of God.

Once I knew in my heart that God really does speak to us, I wanted to hear Him more. I couldn't believe that He would speak to me, a common girl. I thought that hearing God was something only special people got to do. I thought that God had to really love you more than others to give you that gift.

Yet, because He was willing to speak to me, my self-esteem began to improve. I realized He wanted to have a deep relationship with me. The God of the Universe saw me. He heard my heart. He understood me and I felt loved by Him. He chose to trust me with deep secrets. Who cares what anyone else thought about me. The *One* who mattered saw and heard me and spoke to me.

When the Lord told me about Lacey, I believe it was actually what is called in scripture, a *word of knowledge*. First Corinthians 12:8 mentions a word of knowledge as a spiritual gift; however this is the only place in the Bible that it is mentioned. The general teaching of this gift is that it is information not known by you, given by the Holy Spirit to you for your benefit or for the benefit of another. In this case it was to help Lacey.

I believe that the word of knowledge is designed to equip the person who receives it to minister to or pray for someone else, or it is the Lord giving them knowledge to help themselves. In either case, it is new knowledge received from the Lord to help a person.

In John 10:27, Jesus says "My sheep hear my voice and they know me". This entire Bible chapter discusses how Jesus is our Shepherd and that we hear His voice. When Scripture speaks of us hearing God's voice, it speaks of it in terms of Jesus shepherding us personally. He is leading us, guiding us and keeping us out of harm's way.

So, going back to my last year at ORU, the rest of the school year I practiced hearing. I made a regular habit of praying over the girls' doors at night, listening for strong thoughts or *impressions* that might come from the Lord. Sometimes I'd have a one word thought like *fearfulness* come to me as I was praying. I'd know God was giving me knowledge of what to pray for that girl, that she must deal with fearfulness. Other times there was more to it, a much more detailed description of what to pray for. These words of knowledge came, I believe, because I was in spiritual authority over these girls (as their chaplain) and the Lord was equipping me with what I needed to battle for them in prayer. I believe He could trust me not to abuse the information, but to use it to pray. I wasn't going to go tell on anyone or use the information to gossip. It was between God and me for the purpose of more effective prayer over these girls' lives.

Learning that these words of knowledge that the Lord was giving me were coming as thoughts, I was empowered to hear the Lord for my own personal life.

Please know, learning to hear His voice takes time and is a process. Most of the time we don't doubt God, we doubt ourselves. I know I did (and still do). So it takes time and practice.

Words of Knowledge Are Sometimes For Much Later

Life is full of crossroads, especially when you are a young adult. Choices you make during the high school and college years can define much of who you become in years to come. During this time in life you are deciding Very important things like who you might marry and what vocation you will choose. Scripture has pointed out that Jesus is our Shepherd. That means He leads us in the ways we should go. It's so incredibly beneficial to hear God give you directions during these important years of your life.

Later in life, crossroads may come in the form of a crisis or unexpected bumps in the road such as well. Crossroads may come in the form of a crisis or unexpected bumps in the road such as losing a job, relationship problems, or maybe a sick child. Whenever life throws a curve ball, it is very important to be able to hear the Shepherd's advice and get His perspective.

When it comes to finding a mate, some think that there isn't one specific person out there for you, that many people could *work out* as potential mates. That may be true to some degree. But if you have a personal life coach who knows all things and all people and you invite Him into the process, don't you think He knows someone who is best for you? Isn't it possible He can make a way for your paths to cross?

In my case, in high school and college I dated several really great young men who could have *worked out*, yet I specifically asked God to look forward in my life and find that right person. I wanted Him to *pick the very best* man for me.

In the Fall of 1997 I went off to Oral Roberts University. The Sunday before I was to move there, I went to a Sunday night church service at a church in my hometown. They had a special speaker who was visiting that night. I honestly don't remember what he talked about, but after the service he came up to me and had a word of knowledge for me. This preacher claimed to hear God's voice. I didn't know whether to believe him or not. If he was a quack, he had gone off the deep end and was fabricating a message from God to me. At this point in my life I wasn't so sure about things like this, but I was willing to listen and learn. This preacher told me that in one week I would meet my future husband.

What girl wouldn't want to hear something like that! I was excited at the idea. I imagined walking into a classroom and seeing a beam of light settling on *the one*. He'd see me and sparks would fly, fireworks would go off and all would be history.

Reality was much more disappointing. One week later, I moved into the dorms and met many new people. There was no glowing light that appeared over any specific guy as I walked into any of the rooms. So at the time I received it, if it really was a word from the Lord, it didn't do much for me. During my time at school, I'd often wonder if that preacher had been mistaken.

At ORU there are no fraternities or sororities, but instead there are brother and sister wings of the dorms. Each girl's dorm wing had a brother dorm wing and we had social functions together. The brother and sister wings shared an eating area in the cafeteria, so on my first day I sat with and met several of my brotherwingers. One of the guys I met that day, at the lunch table was Erik Selvig.

Erik and I became good friends over the next few years but never thought about dating. It was during Our senior year when Erik went with me on a trip to Chicago for a friend's wedding, that I realized I loved him. He had been a good friend but my feelings had grown stronger. I'll save the complete story for another time, but on that trip he realized the same thing. A year later we were married. By this time I had completely forgotten the preacher's words from years before. It came back to my mind as we were making preparations for our wedding. One day I suddenly realized that I *had* met Erik that first week of school, and the *word* from the preacher had actually been correct! While it hadn't seemed to be a benefit to hear it in the immediate, it was now serving as confirmation that I was walking down the right path, marrying the right man God had intended for me all along.

Words of Knowledge Have Purpose

Words of knowledge either give you specific wisdom you don't have but need, or they equip you to minister or pray for someone else.

I worked at a very large ministry in Colorado Springs for over 10 years. One day I was walking down a hall at work and saw a man that I did not know personally but who worked there, coming towards me. I started to feel physically sick and repulsed towards this man and I heard the Lord tell me (through thoughts) some sinful things that he had been involved in. There was no way I could have known these things on my own. I was either making up a whopper of a story in my head, or God was showing me things that I would have preferred stay hidden in the dark. Anger rose up in my soul towards this man. For days my spirit grieved when thinking of him. I couldn't even look at him. I cried out to the Lord one day while I was driving.

"Why did you show me that?" I asked God out loud. And, "What purpose is there in me knowing that information?" Keep in mind I didn't know the man well enough to approach him. I didn't feel like I was supposed to confront him.

"Why would you reveal such a deep thing to me about a person if there is nothing I can do about it?" I asked.

The Lord spoke to my mind very softly and clearly, "I trusted you with that information so you can pray for my son."

Like a balloon with a fast leak, the air was let out of my disgust immediately. Just in hearing the Lord call him His son, I was humbled as I saw that I had failed to look at him as the Lord did. I did not have *God's perspective* on the situation. Where I saw a sinner deserving judgment and correction, the Lord wanted me to see His hurting child with a big problem. God looked at him with incredible love and I had judged him. God needed me to pray for him.

I kept my mouth silent and never said a word about what the Lord had revealed to me about this man, yet within days the things that the Lord had shown me came out in the public and were confirmed by the evening news.

I am not suggesting that this man should not be subject to the law, or that he shouldn't receive correction by his superiors. However I had placed myself in a judgment position over this man when I didn't have a function to judge him. I was not his superior. I was not an agent of the law. He had not personally sinned against me.

But somehow I had reserved the right to recognize his sin and hold it against him. Because of what the Lord spoke to me, I was able to see God's perspective.

The Lord didn't want me to judge the man. I had failed to recognize him as a brother in the Lord who needed help. I had judged him instead of thinking how I could help to rescue, pray for and help this child of God. How many times do we as Christians do that when a brother or sister falls?

It is a little scary that the Lord reveals a secret to strangers isn't it? I do believe that He told me this man's issues because He wanted me to pray and because He wanted to give me His perspective on the situation. My knee-jerk reaction was to judge the man because I know that God does not approve of the actions he was involved in. But if I wasn't a superior to this man or in a place to correct him, why did I declare myself his judge?

Hearing the Lord speak to my heart about this situation helped me to see that He saw this man as His son. He was interested in helping His son and wanted to include me in that help.

Baby Steps to Developing This Gift

Do you want the Lord to give you words of knowledge? I believe there are some common sense steps you can take to get to the place where you can receive them.

The first step is to learn to hear Him in your own personal life. There really is no difference in the method of hearing Him. When you can clearly hear Him for your own needs, He might start trusting you with the needs of others.

The second step is to be trustworthy, so that the Lord knows He can trust you with the information. He isn't telling you about it so that you can use it to gossip. And if you're not in a place of authority to speak into that person's life, I think you should assume the knowledge is not to be shared with them or others.

Then, I believe you have placed yourself in the position to receive that gift, if He so desires to give it. (1 Corinthians 12:4).

Other Examples of Words of Knowledge:

A friend of mine who works in the television industry wrote to me with this example:

"Just a few days ago, my brother sent me a text about a Christian TV show I was working on. He said that his girlfriend really needed to hear the message of that program. God revealed part of her story to me right there, so to confirm it I asked if she had had an abortion 20 years ago. "How did you know?" he typed. "Sometimes God speaks to me in my mind, & I just know things." I answered.

God revealed a part of this woman's story to my friend to most likely give him compassion for this girl, and to motivate him to get the program to his brother so the girlfriend could hear the message. The Lord wants us to be his body just as we are His hands, and His feet. We are His hands, we are His feet. We take the good news of the gift of salvation to other people around us who simply do not know. God spoke enough of this girl's situation to my friend so that he would be motivated to get the good news of forgiveness and healing to her to a TV program he had access to.

Chapter 4

Why God Speaks

God Speaks to You Because He Loves You Very Much.

God wants to have a relationship with you (Jer. 29:13). He wants to guide your steps (Prov. 3:5). He wants to give you His presence (Ps. 9:1). He wants to be compassionate and bless you (Joel 2:12). He wants to let you know how much of a son or daughter you are (Joel 2:12). He wants to help you see what a true Father is really like (John 3:16). He wants you to discover things and to *taste and see* that He is good (Psalm 34:8).

God speaks to you through your thoughts because He is intimate. His Spirit is poured out upon you (Joel 2:28). He is near (James 4:8) and He has longed for a deeper relationship with you. He does not want to burden you (1 John 5:3). He wants you to love and trust and learn from Him. It's what He has wanted from the beginning of time. It's what He wanted with Adam and Eve and it is what He wanted with all of mankind. Before Adam and Eve took from the tree of the knowledge of good and evil, their knowledge was good. Everything was *good*. God called His finished creation good.

Where did Adam and Eve get their knowledge from before this troublesome tree entered the picture? It's simple. They got it from their relationship with God.

Picture this Father who created a world full of wonder and discovery just so that His children could learn from Him. See Him as He creates atoms and stars and galaxies, thinking of us all along. There was and still is so much to discover, so much to uncover together. I imagine that He saw Himself revealing deep mysteries to us as the human race learned to trust Him and seek His wisdom. He developed deep mysteries for us with the intention of giving us insight as we come to Him to share our wonder and delight in the world He created for us.

It's apparent from Scripture that Adam and Eve took walks through the garden with Him. God wanted to show them everything and watch their wonder and answer their questions. He is the one who designed everything, He has all the answers. We were always supposed to get our knowledge and wisdom from our relationship with Him. That was good. That was the design. He is not a hard taskmaster intent on making us beg for answers, He is a kind Father who wants relationships with His people.

This is what the *big sin* is all about in the garden of Eden! It's not that God didn't want them to eat apples! It's that they made a choice to gain wisdom on their own, without God. They already had access to the perfect wisdom and insight to the universe through the relationship with the Father, yet they chose to pursue wisdom without Him.

God is the one who made the earth. He made the solar system, the trees, the animals, everything. After everything He did to bring us into existence and the good plans He had for us, we chose to try to learn it and explore it without Him. It was like saying, "Hey thanks for making this incredible world for us, but we'll take it from here."

Yet God still pined for a relationship with the people He created and wove a way into the human story to redeem the situation and allow us to restore the relationship. Now, if we want that restored relationship, we must come through the door He provided. We must come through His son Jesus (John 14:6).

God has given us to Jesus (John 10:29). We are His. He is ours. He's our Shepherd. He is our High Priest (Hebrews 8:1) who sacrificed and makes us clean before God. He is the One, the only One, who can make us right again with God.

As we accept Him and His sacrifice which makes us clean, He takes our hand and joins it with the Father's. He teaches us how to pray correctly to the Father. He says to pray like this, "Our Father in Heaven, hallowed be Thy Name…" He is the one who redeems us and brings us back. Then, as the Holy Spirit works in us, we begin to hear the voice of Jesus speaking in our lives and in our thoughts. We slowly learn to trust that we are hearing Him as we see prayers and questions answered. His Spirit teaches us as we trust more and more and even more. As we finally become confident that we do hear the voice of God in our thoughts, we find ourselves back to the way it was supposed to be from the beginning, with the ability to gain Godly insight and wisdom to our carnal knowledge.

God Speaks to Reveal Things About Your Future and to Help You Navigate Your Path.

I have a degree in Bible and Music Ministry and another in Music Composition and Technology. I play the piano and the guitar and I've been writing songs since I was ten years old. During my college years I used to lead worship in school chapel services as well as at a local church. This was my calling I thought, and I wanted to be a worship leader as my vocation.

One day right after my college graduation, I was out on a walk and the Lord spoke to me through a powerful picture in my mind. I saw, a picture of a baseball team. The players were my fellow graduates going out into the world to be worship leaders. I was sitting on the bench. The Lord said to me through a thought, "Wendy, I'm putting you on the bench. You're not going to go be a worship leader right now. Trust Me." I felt as if the wind had been knocked out of me. Worship leading was everything I had hoped for and sought to be. I had dreamed of leading worship for years. It was my passion. It is why I went to college.

Yet I had heard Him and I knew it was Him. Hoping that He knew what He was doing, I put everything regarding worship leading down. I gave away my instruments and trusted God's best for my life.

For the next 15 years I would not sing, play an instrument or lead worship. Every time I tried, the doors would not open and I felt unrest in my heart. Unfortunately during this time I developed a lot of self-doubt and I listened to the voice of the enemy tell me that God did not approve of me as a worship leader.

I don't know the exact reasons God had me sit on the bench, but looking back on the time I have a few suspicions.

During those years I had three children. I also lost three children during failed pregnancies. I went through many bouts of post-partum depression and feelings of being overwhelmed with life. I really think I was in no position to serve as a worship leader with any stability. I think my Shepherd knew I needed to be gently led through those years before letting me run with my passion. I think He had compassion and grace for me in this area, but I can only see that now as I look behind me.

So, one day in 2012 I was driving alone in my car. I heard the Lord speak in my thoughts, "You need to prepare because it's time to come off the bench."

That is all He had to say and I knew exactly what He meant. I knew He was calling me back into worship leading.

I knew I had heard Him. There were times in the years before when I had longed to hear Him say that. I had asked and listened to hear Him say that but He never had. Now, I had adjusted well to the idea of never leading worship again, convinced I had somehow offended God or proved unworthy to fulfill my original calling. I thought He was done with me in that arena. So, I was surprised to hear Him tell me it was time. I hadn't sung or played the piano or guitar in literally 15 years. Why me? Why now?

I decided that I would trust and believe that I had heard Him, but I wouldn't tell anyone about it. I'd just wait and see what happened. I started to look through worship music again and listen to see what was popular. I got my guitar out and started playing a little bit.

A month later I had lunch with my pastor's wife who was getting ready to start a city-wide weekly women's meeting. She told me that she felt she was to ask me to lead the worship. I hadn't even told her very much of my story. We sat over lunch and cried together as I told her that God had just told me it was time to get off the bench.

God Speaks to Encourage People

During my period of 15 years when I was not leading worship, I attended an evening service at my church. We had a special night where my pastor was teaching about spiritual gifts. There was a guest worship leader that night, Darrell Evans. Being a worship leader at heart, I knew of Darrell and the great songs he wrote. He had been leading worship in

Tulsa, OK while I was a student at ORU and it was such a treat for me to be able to see him at my home church in Colorado. During the worship service I was praying and asking God to give me songs again, to let me write music again. I was also about 6 months pregnant with my first baby boy. I was praying and asking God to bless my baby with spiritual gifts as well.

Suddenly, Darrell stopped singing but continued to play his guitar. He had his eyes closed and started to speak. He said, "There's a mom here, and your baby is still in the womb. You've been praying for God to use this child, this baby boy. God is pouring out songs into him even now and he's pouring songs into you. To confirm this, your baby is moving now as we speak." My son jumped in the womb and kicked me as he said this. It was the most awesome and humbling experience.

I didn't know Darrell and hadn't ever met him. He didn't know me or that I was pregnant, let alone that I was pregnant with a baby boy. There were hundreds of people in the audience. He couldn't see me in the darkened room. He didn't know that I had been praying and asking God to use my son and to give him gifts. But the Lord was able to use Darrell to encourage me because Darrell knew how to hear God's voice.

God Speaks to Comfort You in Tragedy.

One of the hardest things I've gone through in life is losing a baby. I've actually lost three. Before I ever lost a child however, I had a vision. It was early in our marriage before we had children. I was at a friend's church and it was during the worship service. Suddenly this image was in my mind very strongly. I didn't understand it, and actually misinterpreted it at the time.

In this picture I saw God the Father sitting on a throne. Erik and I were standing before Him and He took us by the hands and gathered us up on His lap. We looked like children and He was holding and hugging us. Then, I looked down and saw three children standing before the throne. Two girls and a little boy were standing there. The girls were the oldest and the boy the youngest. Jesus, who was sitting on the throne next to the Father, stood up and went and gathered the children into His arms. He looked at us lovingly and with a big smile. He brought them back with Him as he sat on His throne, He held our kids in His arms.

That is all there was. It was so real, I was certain that He had just showed me that I'd have two girls and a boy and we'd all live happily ever after. Yet, the childhood bearing days ahead would become a challenge, and I would eventually lose 3 children during pregnancies. I would carry 3 others to term, but they would be all boys and it didn't make sense that I had seen a vision with girls in it when I ended up having only boys. In hindsight, I am certain that it was those 3 children that I lost whom I saw in the vision, and I am certain that God was showing me that He had my children in His arms. He wanted us to know that they are with Him.

A Vision of Comfort

We were so excited to be pregnant. We had tried for almost a year with no success and then suddenly I was expecting! To add even more joy to the situation, we had found out that a brother and sister-in-law were expecting too! How fun this was going to be! The family was all very excited, but unfortunately the excitement wouldn't last.

A few months later we were devastated to find out that my brother and sister in law had miscarried and lost their child. Now the joy turned to sorrow and pain for the family and we were all very sad.

My mother-in-law, a godly woman, was in prayer a few weeks after this and saw a vision from the Lord. In her prayer time, she saw a picture in her mind of her mother, (who had already passed away and was with the Lord), standing in heaven holding two swaddled babies in her arms. My mother-in-law immediately knew that my child was the second baby. She told me that her first reaction was to rebuke it and say, "No, Wendy's baby will not die in the name of Jesus." But what she didn't know is that the baby already had. We had lost the baby a few days before but hadn't told anyone yet. Why did God speak to my mother-in-law about this? To give her and the rest of us peace that He knew and understood our pain. And, to give us a peace that those children were taken care of. He was giving us hope in a very dark time. Because we were open to hearing His voice He was able to comfort us.

Wendy Selvig

God Speaks to Give Us His Perspective On A Situation.

Erik and I love our pastor. Pastor Ted Haggard really has quite a redemption story to tell. We attended the Mega Church New Life Church in Colorado Springs for 13 years. You may or may not know it was the center of a firestorm of media attention, when our pastor was revealed to be involved in a major scandal. We, like many other people at the church, were shaken to our core when it all happened. I encourage everyone to read Ted's wife's book, *Why I Stayed*, by Gayle Haggard, if you are interested in the full story.

Had I not been able to hear God's voice, I don't know where I would be standing today on how I feel about him. Scandals are difficult things and a lot of people have a hard time forgiving when a leader falls. Thankfully, the Lord spoke to me before the scandal even hit and His voice gave me perspective when the storm came.

The Sunday before the scandal broke out, I saw our pastor walk down the aisle towards the platform with the other pastors as he always did, right as the service was about to start.

The Lord spoke to me through a very strong thought and what I can only describe as strong gripping emotions when I saw him. The thought was God's voice in my head very strongly saying, "Assassination attempt on Pastor Ted this week," and I assumed that there would be a literal assassination attempt of some kind on his life.

Not only had God spoken a thought in my head, it was also accompanied by a strong emotion. At this point in my life I wasn't sure of myself when I heard God speak. I certainly wasn't looking to hear from God on this and when I heard it I was shocked. I questioned and doubted but was starting to know the difference between my own thoughts and God's. I knew I had heard His voice on this. I just wasn't sure what to do with it.

At that time, I didn't have any sort of relationship with pastor Ted. I certainly had no reason for him to allow me to speak into His life. So, I knew God didn't expect me to tell him what I had heard. Instead I assumed I was to pray for him, to indeed pray for his life.

That following Thursday, something traumatic did happen with our pastor, though not what I expected. A major scandal was uncovered. The entire church including my husband and I were reeling in shock from it.

And while his story is long and this is not the place to tell it all, his life as he knew it then was forever changed.

All the accomplishments, the books and the leadership he had provided, were all buried under the scandal. Trust with people had been broken, hearts were confused, and he found himself in a place where suicidal thoughts kept him company day by day. Had he succumbed at this weak point, truly everything in his life would have been destroyed.

Had I not clearly heard the voice of the Lord speak to me about an assassination attempt of the enemy, I would not have known how the Lord wanted me to view the situation. I may have chosen to judge him with anger and unforgiveness, because I was so deeply hurt over the situation.

During this emotional time my husband and I needed perspective. We needed to know how God was viewing the situation. Was God angry at our pastor and judging him? Was this an unpardonable sin that should render him unable to serve in ministry ever again? Should we forgive him or had he been deceiving us all along and could he ever be trusted again? These were questions we had to process during this time. God's perspective helped us wade through these waters.

Following the scandal, Pastor Ted went through intense counseling for some abuse and traumatic things that had happened in his life that he had never worked through. He publicly repented and asked for forgiveness. Yet the word of the Lord gave me perspective so that I would know what to think about my pastor when I wasn't sure on my own. I hadn't heard "getting what he deserves" from the Lord, I had heard, "assassination attempt." It's all in the perspective.

I'm not saying that he shouldn't have been corrected by the men who were in authority over him. I'm not saying that he didn't hurt people, or that he shouldn't have had to apologize or get help. He definitely needed to do those things, and he did.

I am saying that because I wasn't in direct authority over him or in a trusted relationship with him, I should not have been judging, I should have been helping.

Many people are still not able to forgive him. Some people walk around years later with poison on their tongue and in their hearts. Had they been able to get God's perspective on the situation, I believe they'd be walking free in their hearts towards him today.

Later, several years after the scandal, the Lord showed me that my pastor is like the prodigal son, whom He loves. Even though his son fell and shamed his name, the father rejoiced and restored authority to his son by placing his coat on him when he returned. He didn't make him come in through the back door and be a servant (which the son offered to do), He restored him to position and authority.

There are people who think Pastor Ted should return to the church humbly, slipping in the back door and not ever be in a position of authority again. But according to the prodigal son story, that is how the jealous older brother saw things, not the Father. It's all in who's perspective you want to view things.

Knowing God's perspective and how He saw my pastor helped me to see how God wanted me to see him. And it put me in a position of being able to forgive and give grace to my pastor as he walked through his restoration in the following years.

God Speaks to Help You Avoid Disaster

I worked for many years at Focus on the Family, a large radio ministry in Colorado Springs. I was the producer for a national live call in talk show for women. We had a high profile host, and the pressure was high because we were a live national radio program. If we had a technical problem, hundreds of thousands of people heard us. So I tried to always be on my toes when it came to preparing for the show.

One day I was praying for an upcoming broadcast and the Lord spoke to me. Our host was not in studio with us, she was in Washington D.C. and connected to us through something called an ISDN line. The Lord told me that the ISDN line was going to drop at the end of the show and that we wouldn't have time to reconnect with our host. The show would be over without an ending. That would be bad for national broadcasting, and bad for my job.

I trusted what He said to me and I contacted our host. I told her that she was going to think it strange, but that I needed her to record a one minute ending to the show that we could use as a backup in case we ever lost her connection near the end of the show. She did think I was a little crazy, but she agreed to record it for me. The next day when we were live, I had her recorded ending cued up and ready to go. Amazingly like clockwork, that ISDN line dropped our host during the last commercial and we had no time to reconnect with her and end the show correctly. I brought in some music, hit "play" on the prerecorded ending, and nobody knew we had lost our host. The Lord was so faithful and He cared about helping us avoid disaster. My Shepherd gently guided me through what would have been a stressful and failure-filled day, into peace, confidence and success! High five Jesus!

Chapter 5

The Voice of An Enemy

A Spiritual War

It doesn't really matter if you believe in gravity or not, the laws of physics pull you down if you step off a cliff.

The same goes for the spiritual realm. Whether you believe in it or not, there's a lot going on right under our noses that we can't see with our physical eyes. As it says in 1 Corinthians 13:12, "For now we see only a reflection as in a mirror; then we shall see face to face. Now I know in part; then I shall know fully, even as I am fully known."

One of the things Scripture does tell us is that we are in a spiritual war. Ephesians 6:12 says, "Our struggle is not against flesh and blood, but against the rulers, against the authorities, against the powers of this dark world and against the spiritual forces of evil in the heavenly realms."

According to tradition, Satan was an angel who rebelled and was cast out of heaven. He apparently became prideful and arrogant in his beauty and status and desired to be worshiped as God. Because of his pride, God removed him from his exalted position and role. "How you have fallen from heaven, O morning star, son of the dawn! You have been cast down to the earth, you who once laid low the nations!"(Isaiah 14:12). In the book of Revelation, Satan is "a star that had fallen from the sky to the earth" (Revelation 9:1).

One third of "thousands upon thousands of angels" (Hebrews 12:22) rebelled with him. He was hurled to the earth and his angels with him"

(Revelation 12:3-9). War breaks out in heaven and "the dragon and his angels fought back" (Revelation 12:7).

Some believe demons to be the fallen angels, and others believe them to be something else (which will be explained a little later in this chapter). Scripture tells us that the enemy, Satan, is the *god of this age* (2 Corinthians 4:4) and that he is here to lie (John 8:44), steal, kill and destroy (John 10:10). He wants to steal the blessings and benefits that God has for us. He'd like to kill you, steal from you and cause your life to run short of the blessings you are promised, and he wants to destroy every good work of the Father in your life. He's called the *Father of Lies* and he will lie to you to accomplish any of these things. You truly do have an enemy.

The Voice of Your Enemy, Satan and his Demons: Follow the Worship

"(Satan) was a murderer from the beginning, not holding to the truth, for there is no truth in him. When he lies, he speaks his native language, for he is a liar and the father of lies."-John 8:44

Satan is defeated by the cross of Christ. But in understanding Satan you must understand where we are on the timeline of eternity. He has been defeated and will be cast into a lake of fire for all eternity, but right now He is still at large. We are in the age that he has been called the god of (2 Corinthians 4:4). He's still present on the earth and has power to steal, kill and destroy. Here are a few facts about Satan according to Scripture.

1. Satan knows and uses Scriptures to promote false doctrine and deceptions (Matthew 4:1-11).
2. He plants his people in the Kingdom. (Matt. 13:38-39).
3. He takes away the Word of God from the hearts of some people (Luke 8:10-13).
4. He puts into the heart of men to do evil even to the extent of betraying the Son of God (John 13:2).
5. He can oppress some to the point that they need healing. (Acts 10:38-39)
6. He has schemes against us. (Ephesians 6:11-12)

7. He is able to ensnare and hold people captive to do his will (II Timothy 2:25-26).
8. He deceives and is capable of deceiving the whole world (Rev 12:8-9).
9. He can enter into some people (Luke 22:3).
10. He can sift people like sifting wheat (Luke 22:31-33)
11. He has power to keep people in darkness (Acts 26:16-18).
12. He has angels (Rev. 12:8-9).
13. He can have schemes against us. (II Cor 2:10-11).
14. He disguises himself as an angel of light (II Cor 11:14-15).
15. Satan hinders us at times (I Thes 2:17-18).
16. "Power," "Signs," and "False Wonders" can be performed by Satan (II Thes 2:9-10).

Scripture suggests that Satan was designed by God to be a worship leader in heaven (Ezekiel 28:12-17 and Isaiah 14:12-14). Though he is cast to earth (and god of this world, 1 Corinthians 4:4), I believe he still is a worship leader by nature. In Matthew 4:9, he tempted Jesus to worship him.

As for the human race, Satan tries to lead us to worship anything that is not God. He hates God. He hates you and he wants to hurt and destroy you (1 Peter 5:8).

So, to recognize your enemy speaking, you have to know the heart of your enemy. The heart of your enemy, will be promoting the worship or glorification of anything but God.

Giants and Demons Who Speak

Ok, hold onto your hat because we're about to dive down a crazy sounding, Alice-in-Wonderland-type of rabbit hole. Many believe that the fallen angels are demons, and they very well may be. Yet there is another theory which I believe adds an interesting layer to the idea of a *demon*. At first, this theory sounded *out there* to me until I started doing research on it and found some hard evidence that opened my mind a bit.

This is my son Erik. He and I travelled to South Africa to view this ancient giant footprint that is in pure granite. We touched it and felt the hardened lava that squeezed up between the toes. We felt the curvature of the arch. It truly is a footprint of a very large person from ancient times.

This theory has to do with real live giant people. Giants are one of the cornerstones of the myths and traditions of almost every culture on Earth. The Greeks and Romans had their Titans, the Hindus have their Daityas. The Norse had frost giants, and the Celtic had the Fomors. Many more giants are woven into ancient stories from around the world.

In a crazy, conspiracy theory-sounding idea, there is evidence that many of the archeological discoveries of giants have been suppressed. Very large skeletons have been found around the world as well as footprints that have been captured in granite. I've been to personally see one of the footprints in South Africa and it was quite amazing. I read people's comments online about how the footprint could be something that was formed by nature and how it could be a natural phenomenon that just appeared to look like a footprint. But once I saw it with my own eyes, there was no doubt it was a real footprint. You could feel the arch of the foot and where the lava had squeezed up between the toes and hardened. There also are a few museums left around the world that display giant bones. There is hard evidence of these giant people, but strangely they are not talked about in today's scientific circles.

So what do giants have to do with demonic spirits? Let's start with a quote from an ancient text. "Evil spirits have proceeded from their bodies; because they are born from men and from the holy Watchers (angels) is their beginning and primal origin; they shall be evil spirits on earth, and evil spirits shall they be called. And the spirits of the *giants* afflict, oppress, destroy, attack, do battle, and work destruction on the earth, and cause trouble: they take no food, but nevertheless hunger and thirst, and cause offences. And these spirits shall rise up against the children of men and against the women, because they have proceeded from them." –The Book of Enoch, 15:8

The Book of Enoch is ascribed to Enoch, the great-grandfather of Noah. There is a lot of controversy on the authenticity of this book, so please feel free to take this with a grain of salt. Enoch is the one person who was taken by God and *was no more*. This book is not regarded as part of the Canon of Scripture. It is an ancient book, but not Scripture. However before you discredit it, you should know a few things about it.

"The Aramaic Book of Enoch very considerably influenced the idiom of the New Testament and patristic literature, more so in fact than any other writing of the Apocrypha and Pseudepigrapha." - Norman Golb, Who Wrote the Dead Sea Scrolls? (1995) p. 366

"Chapters 1-36, The Book of the Watchers may date from the third century BCE. Parts of its text have been identified on several copies from Qumran cave 4; the earliest fragmentary manuscript (4QEnocha) dates, according to the editor J.T. Milk, to between 200 and 150 BCE. All Qumran copies are in the Aramaic language." - James C. Vanderkam

A short section of 1 Enoch (1En1:9) is quoted in the New Testament (Letter of Jude 1:14-15), and there it is attributed to *Enoch the Seventh from Adam* (1En 60:8).

It is argued that all the writers of the New Testament were familiar with it and were influenced by it in thought and diction. I don't consider it equal with Scripture, but I do regard it as a fascinating text that Jesus knew about and it was referenced to in Scripture. I think it is worth considering.

The Book of Enoch has some pretty wild stuff in it and is fascinating to me. It talks a lot about the history of the earth and mankind. It talks about the origin of demons and spirits, and as I studied this, the demons sounded a lot like what people today think of as *ghosts*. According to this book, when the *sons of God* (understood as fallen angels) took wives from the *daughters of men* in Genesis (Genesis 6:4), there was a defiled race of part angels/part humans (called Nephilim). They were larger than typical humans and called *giants*.

These unions were not sanctioned by God and were done in direct disobedience to the will of God for the earth. This text says these children were evil and did all kinds of terrible things like consuming all of the resources and then killing and eating humans. The fallen angels apparently presented themselves to humans as *gods* and so their children, these giants, had the blood of *the gods* in them. Does any of this ring a bell? Many ancient cultures claim their kings are children of *the gods*. Many carvings and hieroglyphics show giants as their leaders too.

This race of beings were the *giants of old* and are mentioned in the Bible. These Enochian texts say that God's punishment on the fallen angels was dire for the souls of their giant children. When these children died, their spirits would roam the earth forever with no promise of resurrection.

While the children of men have a promise of resurrection, the fallen angels' children do not have that promise. The Book of Enoch says, "the spirits of the giants afflict, oppress, destroy, attack, do battle, and work destruction on the earth, and cause trouble." Sounds like a demon to me.

A few years ago I watched a popular TV show called Ghost Hunters. The hunters would go into so-called haunted houses and try to provoke spirits to see if anything dwelled there. Sometimes they'd get no response at all, and sometimes they would. They used recorders that would pick up voices that their ears didn't pick up on. Sometimes a Ghost Hunter would hear a noise but when you amplified the sound wave, you could hear (and visually see on the sound wave via computer) a voice within the noise. I've personally done work with audio and sound waves, so this interested me.

The voice recorded but not heard by the naked ear often spoke directly to the Ghost Hunter. Sometimes the Ghost Hunter would be named by name. Things would be said like, "I want you to leave John"...or profanities were spoken.

To me, that means these spirits are speaking to people. If this is real, they have found a frequency that our ears don't hear but our minds still pick up on. What a great way to "cause offenses without being seen."

Whether you believe the Enoch account or if you think a demon is something else, in all accounts, they aren't good. If demons are speaking to you, you can't hear them with your physical ears, but it appears they are speaking.

I personally believe that since they are spirits, they speak directly to our spirits. Our minds then interpret the voice as a thought. If you are unaware of this process, you will just think that every thought is your own. And the evil spirit gets to cause an offense "without being observed."

If a demon can whisper to you and make you think it's words are your own thoughts, how powerful a tool is that to someone who hates you and wants to destroy your life?

You have hope and a promise from God. If you ask and accept the free gift, You get what the evil spirits will never have – salvation and resurrection. You were created with a purpose, to have a relationship with God. They were punished by their evil actions (recorded in the book of Enoch) and will wander the earth forever without bodies. They are full of hate, are deceivers, and want to influence you. So if demons are trying to speak to you and influence you, let's discuss what some of those thoughts might be:

"There is no God."

"You live and die and that is all. Live for yourself while you can and enjoy everything you can while you are alive, whether it is beneficial to others or not."

"If there was a God, he must be an old ogre up in the sky that doesn't want you to have fun."

"Science is separate from believing in God. God and Science can't coexist."

"God is a crutch."

"I am my own God. I can do everything on my own. I don't need a God. Christians are stupid."

"God wants to keep good things from you."

Personal Attacks:

"Cancer? You won't survive it. You're going to die."
"Long life? Forget it, statistics are against you."
"Live a prosperous life? Not hardly. Only those born into wealth get to live like that."
"You are so fat."
"You aren't pretty."
"Nobody wants to be your friend."
"That person is so rude. I hate her."
"I'd be better off dead."
"I hope he gets what he deserves."
"I HATE...."
"I DESERVE..."
"I NEED..."
And on, and on, and on.... Negative, negative, negative thoughts.

Taking Every Thought Captive

The Bible instructs us to 'take every thought captive." (2 Cor. 10:3-5)

To know the origin of the different thoughts in your head, you will have to question the heart (or intent) of the thought. And if this sounds exhausting, remember James 4:7: "Submit yourselves, then, to God. Resist the devil, and he will flee from you."

As you begin to recognize that the negativity is coming from the demonic realm and not from yourself, you can resist those thoughts. Resist them with a simple, "In the name of Jesus, no." You can reject the thoughts, in the name of Jesus. An entire book could be written on what "in the name of Jesus" means, but to simplify, as a Christian, you speak in Christ's authority. Jesus conquered the devil and his followers and they have to obey Him. If you know the authority you walk in, and speak in His name, they have to obey you too.

Since the demons like to cause trouble *without being observed*, when you recognize the source of the thoughts and resist them in Jesus' name, their game is up. As you resist those thoughts, they will eventually flee from you and go bother someone else who is easier to fool. You'll find the evil and derogatory thoughts happening less and less. They like to come back every once in a while to test and see if you still can recognize them, but keep resisting those thoughts and eventually they go away.

Negativity, hatred, pride and the worship of anything but God comes from the evil spirits who have set themselves as your enemies.

For more study on the topic of giants, I recommend the following resources:

1. *Genesis 6 Giants, Master Builders of Prehistoric and Ancient Civilizations*, by Stephen Quayle. Also, Steve's website has a lot of good information: www.genesis6giants.com
2. *Discovering Ancient Giants*, by William A. Hinson
3. *The Ancient Giants Who Ruled America, The Missing Skeletons and the Great Smithsonian Cover-Up*, by Richard J. Dewhurst
4. *Giants, Sons of the Gods*, by Douglas Van Dorn

He Who is in You is Stronger Than the Enemy

If you trust and believe in Jesus and have asked Him to be your Lord, He has sealed you with His Holy Spirit. That means that He lives *in* you. That means that He has better access to speaking to you than anyone else. Remember the scripture, "He who is in you is greater than he who is in the world." (1 John 4:4)?

He often reminds me when I am worrying about what voice I am hearing that He is much stronger than the enemy and I do hear Him.

Chapter 6

The Voice of God

God's Voice

"*God is not a man, that he should lie, nor a son of man, that he should change his mind. Does he speak and then not act? Does he promise and not fulfill?*" –Numbers 23:19

God is a truth teller. He loves truth. *"Make them holy by your truth; teach them your word, which is truth."* –John 17:17 You will find that His character is in sharp contrast with the enemy's. That makes it pretty easy to determine who is speaking, as long as you know the truth of God's Word to compare the thought to, and God's intent and posture towards you.

I love reading the Old Testament. My husband thinks I'm crazy (of course his major in college was the New Testament, so he may be biased). But I love reading the Old Testament because I feel like I get insights into God's character there. But truthfully, the Old Testament is an Old Covenant. One thing that many in the Church seem to fail to understand is that God canceled the Old Covenant in order to make the New Testament valid. That statement may step on a lot of toes, but it's right there in Hebrews 10:9. Speaking of the Old Covenant He says, "See, I have come to do your will. He *takes away the first* in order to establish the second." The Old Covenant is done. It has been taken away. The New Covenant does not complete the Old Testament in that we now follow them both. That is not scriptural! He had to take away the first covenant to establish the second. The second is better; the second one is for our time in history.

It doesn't mean that you shouldn't read or get anything out of the Old Testament; it just means that the laws presented in it no longer apply. It had to be taken away to establish the new. The new has come, in the flesh.

So, if you are trying to figure out God, reading the Old Testament alone is not going to help you on many fronts. In the Old Testament, God had a different posture towards us. The Old Covenant required blood sacrifices to gain us access to God. The Holy Spirit did not live within us at that time either. God wanted for us to be redeemed and made right. He brought a new and better Covenant where the requirements for us to be redeemed are fulfilled in Jesus. God's posture towards us has changed. Instead of servants, we are sons. We are forgiven. We are seen through the sacrifice of Jesus and now stand justified before God. This is the "Good News!" It's all been done! God's posture towards us is loving kindness. We are in a dispensation of grace and authority has been given to us to bind and loose the things in this world (Matthew 18:18).

So when we trust Jesus as our Savior, God puts His Holy Spirit within us and His Spirit speaks wisdom into our minds. Second Corinthians 6:16 has one of the greatest promises from the Lord to believers; "I will dwell in them and walk among them. I will be their God, and they shall be My people." He lives in us. He can and does speak to us! God wants to live in and dwell among us! Paul further builds on this thought in Ephesians 2:22 with we "are being built together for a dwelling place of God in the Spirit."

His words always reflect truth. Your mind hears the thoughts and has to interpret if it is God speaking or not. When your mind is renewed by knowing the Word of God, it can recognize the voice of God in an instant by comparing it to the Word it already knows.

Here are a few scriptures to help you recognize the characteristics God's words will have when He is speaking to you.

Love (1 Corinthians 13:4) Love is patient, love is kind. It does not envy, it does not boast, it is not proud. (1 John 4:8) Whoever does not love does not know God, because God is love.

Joy (Galatians 5:22) But the fruit of the Spirit is love, joy, peace, patience, kindness, goodness, faithfulness,

Peace (Colossians 3:15) Let the peace of Christ rule in your hearts, since as members of one body you were called to peace. And be thankful.

Patience (Romans 12:12) Be joyful in hope, patient in affliction, faithful in prayer.

Kindness (Ephesians 4:32) Be kind and compassionate to one another, forgiving each other, just as in Christ God forgave you.

Fearlessness (2 Timothy 1:7) For God did not give us a spirit of timidity, but a spirit of power, of love and of self-discipline.

Grace (James 4:6) But he gives us more grace. That is why Scripture says: "God opposes the proud but gives grace to the humble."

Holy (Heb 7:26) He is the kind of high priest we need because he is holy and blameless, unstained by sin. He has been set apart from sinners and has been given the highest place of honor in heaven.

Hospitality (Romans 12:13) Share with God's people who are in need. Practice hospitality.

Loyalty (Proverbs 17:17) A friend loves at all times, and a brother is born for adversity. *Note: He has called us His friends! (1 John 3:1)

Perseverance (Galatians 6:9) And let us not grow weary of doing good, for in due season we will reap, if we do not give up.

Supportive (Galatians 6:2) Bear one another's burdens, and so fulfill the law of Christ.

Tactful (Colossians 4:6) Let your speech always be gracious, seasoned with salt, so that you may know how you ought to answer each person.

Tolerant (1 Thes. 5:14) And we urge you, brothers, admonish the idle,[a] encourage the fainthearted, help the weak, be patient with them all.

Understanding (Psalm 90:12) Teach us to number our days, that we may gain a heart of wisdom.

Virtuous (Colossians 3:12-17) Put on then, as God's chosen ones, holy and beloved, compassionate hearts, kindness, humility, meekness, and patience, bearing with one another and, if one has a complaint against another, forgiving each other; as the Lord has forgiven you, so you also must forgive. And above all these put on love, which binds everything together in perfect harmony. And let the peace of Christ rule in your hearts, to which indeed you were called in one body. And be thankful. Let the word of Christ dwell in you richly, teaching and admonishing one another in all wisdom, singing psalms and hymns and spiritual songs, with thankfulness in your hearts to God. And whatever you do, in word or deed, do everything in the name of the Lord Jesus, giving thanks to God the Father through him.

This is in no way an exhaustive list, but simply a guide to see how wonderful the characteristics of God are and what His voice should reflect in your life. His posture towards you is favorable. He will not speak fear or harm to you. Know the intent of your enemy and that of your God, and rightly discern and take captive all the thoughts that enter your mind.

Learning to Hear His Voice

"The Lord is near to all who call on him, to all who call on him in truth." (Psalms 145:18)

"No one whose hope is in you will ever be put to shame..." (Psalms 25:3)

If you're trying to hear His voice and you call on Him to speak to you, He promises to be near. If you're hoping to hear Him, you won't be embarrassed or shamed. Be encouraged. He will come through. He will speak and you will learn to hear Him.

And Jesus came up and spoke to them, saying, *"All authority has been given to Me in heaven and on earth."* –Matthew 28:18

He truly is in authority over your enemy and wants to help you walk in His authority as well. His voice and the enemy's voice can clearly be discerned by looking at the heart/intent/posture behind the thoughts.

Discerning Between Your Own Voice and God's

One of the biggest questions people ask in regards to hearing God's voice is how to know the difference between our own voice and God's. In fact, the biggest hurdle I have had in finishing this book was deciding how to write about this topic.

I have a friend who was a pastor of a very large church. He told me that when he and his staff were praying about their building project they received hundreds of letters and comments from people who claimed to have *heard from the Lord* regarding the direction they should take. Many of the *words* were different, and it lowered his faith in man's ability to hear God speaking. So what happened here? Let's explore it and find out. To get the answers we need, we have to go back to the garden.

Our Spirits Were Designed To Get Wisdom From God

First, let me lay some ground. We are spirit beings (Numbers 16:22) that live in a fallen (Genesis 3:1-24), earthly (Genesis 2:7) body. We were created to be in relationship with our Father. Just as the Holy Spirit and Jesus are in triune relationship with God the Father (1 John 5:7), they have invited us to be a part of that relationship (Ephesians 2:18). Its spirit-to-spirit communication (Romans 8:14), and we are now connected to God in this way, receiving wisdom (James 1:5) from God when we need it. This design was created by God and it is good. The Holy Spirit is poured out and we are sealed with Him (Ephesians 1:13). His Spirit now resides in us and can speak to us at any time.

When we are born into the world, we know nothing. We are blank slates. We need to gain wisdom to grow and mature. I believe the human being is typically always in a state of wanting to grow in wisdom.

When Adam and Eve were in the garden, they were instructed not to eat from the tree of the knowledge of good and evil. Why do you suppose that is? Could it be because they already had access to a more perfect way of learning? Could the tree of good and evil be a step down from what they already had? God had called everything "good" in the garden and they were now choosing "good and evil."

Wendy Selvig

Two Plus Two is Four, Except When It's Five

This is my opinion on what the tree of the knowledge of good and evil represents. *Pure logic devoid of insight from God* comes from the tree of the knowledge of good and evil. It can be correct in and of itself, or it can be wrong because it is missing insight from the One who created everything.

Two flatworms plus two flatworms equals four flatworms, except if you cut one in half. If you do that, you won't have three flatworms and one dead flatworm, you will have five worms, because flatworms regenerate from both ends.

For the person who goes by logic only, they would have stopped at two plus two equals four. For the person with relational insight from the One who created flatworms AND math, you understand that sometimes two plus two can be five.

When Eve saw that the fruit of the tree was good for food and pleasing to the eye, and also desirable for gaining wisdom, she took some of it and ate it. (Genesis 3:6)

The fruit was desirable for gaining wisdom. Yet according to Genesis she already had access to perfect wisdom from her relationship with God the Father. By desiring the fruit that gave wisdom, she was choosing to learn without God's insight or help. She had believed the lie that there was more, that she could be wise on her own without God.

Her husband also ate the fruit, and the two were about to find out what a life with logic but no insight from the Creator would be like.

The curses that came on them involved their physical bodies. The man would no longer have insight from God when it came to tending the earth; he would learn by hard knocks and the sweat of his brow how to grow food. The woman would not give birth easily now, but through a fallen state and without insight into the process from the One who made the process, childbirth would be a painful thing. Their life tasks would no longer be easy. Under the curse, which is basically life without God and His wisdom, they would have to figure things out on their own, which is the hard way of doing things.

The Lord God said, "The man has now become like one of us, knowing good and evil." Apparently, before this sinful act, man only knew good. We were supposed to be connected to God in spirit from the beginning, knowing His goodness and wisdom and life, and probably living forever in that state (because Genesis 3:23 tells us there was a tree of life).

So now, the human race is born into this *fallen* state, relying only on our logic to learn. We are born without the perfect insight of God, without the relationship. The relationship has to be restored or "born again" before we have access to God's wisdom again.

The intimate relationship with God was severed back with Adam and Eve, and so God introduced a plan to save mankind from this broken relationship. He sends Jesus to die as a sacrifice to pay the price for the sin of mankind, and to restore us to a right relationship with God again. "For God so loved the world that He gave his only son, that whoever believes in Him will not perish, but have eternal life." (John 3:16) So if you believe in Jesus, and receive his sacrifice to cover your sinfulness, the Bible says you qualify to eat from that tree of eternal life now! It also says your spirit is born again! (John 1:12-12, Ezekiel 11:19)

What is it to have a born again spirit? This new spirit is in communion with God again, just like Adam and Eve's were before the fall! Because "My sheep hear my voice and I know them (John 10:27)," you now have access to His insight on all things. You are connected to the good wisdom of God, yet you still have knowledge of the evil. That is, you still have the ability to choose logic without God's insight over hearing from the One who created it all.

God is in you and you are in Him. He speaks to your spirit and gives you wisdom, but your brain still can choose to make logical decisions without His insight. Until the end of this age, this will be our plight! We will have to choose between God's wisdom and man's wisdom. This is why we must learn how to clearly discern the voice of God within our minds, so that we can consistently walk in God's good knowledge.

Back To Taking Every Thought Captive

The Bible instructs us to 'take every thought captive." (2 Cor 10:3-5). Every thought must be analyzed and before you decide to share with someone something you think God has said to you, you need to analyze and put the thoughts to the test to make sure you are truly relaying something God has spoken.

At the church where my pastor friend received conflicting *words from God* from people in the congregation regarding their building project, I believe many of those people weren't hearing the voice of God. I think they were offering opinions based on logic devoid of God's insight. In other words, they were resting on logic without relational input from God.

Without clearly hearing the voice of God, their opinions made sense to their minds and they probably thought that if it *made sense logically to them*, it was God showing them the way it should be done.

In addition to mishearing, many who spoke up weren't in authority over or in a position to speak into the pastor's life on this matter. They shouldn't have offered opinion as a *Word of God*. Opinion is always fine to share, but there is a big difference between a logical opinion and a divinely inspired *word* from God.

The Voice of Your Own Soul

When it comes to hearing the difference between our own voice and God's, because we are still in a fallen state, I would say that our own voice *is a combination of our logic without God's insight and anything in us that has been restored by the work of the Holy Spirit.* If a person has rejected Christ and is not a believer, they are walking in pure logic without Godly insight. If a person has accepted that Jesus is God's son and invited Him into their lives, they are in a process of renewal and restoration and our own thoughts will reflect where we are in that process.

We are information gatherers. As humans, we are born without knowledge. We do not know who we are or who God is from birth. At the beginning we have no voice (except to scream when we are not comfortable!) We only know physical desire and discomfort and as we grow we naturally try to feed the first and starve the second.

It is my opinion that as we grow, we gather information and then decide to either accept it or disregard it. If we accept it, we take it in and it becomes a part of us. If that information comes in without any insight from our Father who created the world, then the information is purely logical and sometimes wrong. We form opinions based on the knowledge we have brought in and over time, those opinions represent our own voice. We become a reflection of the information we have gathered and accepted.

As time goes on we find out who we are based on what we have discovered that we like and dislike, what we agree on and disagree on. That is part of the discovery of life! We were originally designed to walk through that process in relationship with the Father, so that He could give us Godly insight in our discovery. The process was supposed to be a joy! It was supposed to be exciting! We were supposed to discover Him and ourselves all at the same time!

Instead, without His insight, we go around calling two plus two as four when sometimes it is five. In our human logic devoid of God's insight, we run into dead ends, things that don't make sense, and have overall frustrated lives. In our blindness we shake our fist at God and say, "Where are you? Life is not fair!"

But when the relationship with God is restored in a person, crooked paths are made straight. Mountains and valleys can be leveled (figuratively). Dead ends can become new beginnings. And when things are hard, we have a Shepherd to guide us to the still waters.

As we study the Word of God and find out more about who He is, the Holy Spirit begins going through the layers of who we are, formed over the years. He gives us the wisdom of God to help correct the things that were learned incorrectly.

He churns up parts of your life that were developed through knowledge without God's insight (wisdom from the tree of the knowledge of good and evil) and He inserts His insight so that you can be healed and restored. It's a process that could take the rest of your life, but it is a process of healing that restores you to who you were supposed to be. If you grew up in a denominational church, you may have heard the term sanctification. That is what this process is called.

If you have learned to recognize God's voice by knowing His Word, His posture towards us, and His character, and you've learned to recognize the negativity of the enemy, everything in between can be counted as your own thoughts – because your thoughts reflect both the evil things that have not been renewed yet and the good things that have been restored by the Word and the Holy Spirit. Until we have our new resurrected bodies, we will reflect a mix of good *and* evil, hopefully ever increasing with the good!

Recap:

The Enemy's voice: Causes harm, fear, panic, no peace, doubt, negativity. It can pursue the worship of other things.

Your own voice: Logic and opinion based on information you've gathered and accepted throughout life. Can be good, can be evil. We've eaten from the tree of the knowledge of good and evil so we have both dry logic and inspired wisdom to choose from.

God's Voice: In line with the Word of God, peace (or lack of it) comes with it. It is loving in nature towards you, and can include wisdom that you are unaware of on your own. This is the voice to focus on and learn to recognize the most.

Renewing Your Mind is the Key

> *"Do not conform any longer to the pattern of this world, but be transformed by the renewing of your mind. Then you will be able to test and approve what God's will is -- his good, pleasing and perfect will (Romans 12:2).*

Our mind is the filter that all voices and thoughts come through. It is in our minds that we tend to make mistakes in hearing God's voice. Sometimes when we err, it is not that we didn't hear Him, it is that we didn't know what to do with what we heard. Or, we were unable to discern between God's voice and the enemy's voice and we attributed to God what came from the mouth of the serpent.

Our filter has to be renewed with the Word of God to appropriately filter both the good and the evil. The more you study the Bible and especially the New Testament, the more you will be able to rightly discern the thoughts in your mind and their origins.

Chapter 7

Hearing God Through Emotionally Charged and Tumultuous Times

A few years ago Erik and I bought a house. I had forgotten how hard it can be to have confidence in what you have heard from God when you're facing an emotional battle. There can be a lot of stress involved in the house-buying process.

For me it was hard because I was emotionally involved. I fell in love with the house immediately and let my emotions get wrapped up in the purchase. I imagined our furniture in the house. I imagined our children playing in their new rooms. I rejoiced at a place big enough to hold our very large extended family. It had become a part of our family already in my mind. And so every time we heard bad news about the loan process, my emotions would get dashed upon the rocks of fearfulness and I would get really upset.

If I feel this way about a house, I can only imagine how hard it is when a loved one is faced with a deathly illness. Or how about losing a home to foreclosure and not knowing where you will land. Tough situations call for hearing God's voice clearly. These kinds of situations are what are called *storms of life*, and we all have times where we venture into these waters.

Regarding the house, before we got far into the loan process I went before the Lord in prayer about it. He spoke to me about the house, assuring me it was going to be ours. And even though I knew that I had heard, I was still very tempted to be tossed about by the emotional waves every time something took a turn for the worse. His words were the anchor that I held onto whenever I heard that the loan might not go through, or that a creditor wasn't responding to a request.

Had I not heard from Him, the stress from the process might have dashed me to pieces. That may sound extreme, but we had been trying to buy a house for years. Just one year before, we were buying a different house and the deal had all fallen through three days before closing. We lost the deal and had to find a place to rent immediately. It was stressful and heartbreaking. It was not a fun experience and I was so afraid of that happening again.

Here are the words from the Lord that I wrote in my journal that anchored me from the storm: "I WILL make crooked paths straight. I will make mountains into valleys and valleys into straight walking paths. Watch me Wendy as I do this for you. Will you then believe that I am really here? That I really love you? That I really want to meet with you on a daily basis? Will you finally see that I am a mighty warrior and that I can make these things so, by saying them? I say it. It is SO. This house is the Selvig family house. Not to be touched by the enemy in any way. Not to have influence from worldly men or angry evil spirits. I'm setting a perimeter around the house, fresh and new. No evil will prevail past the perimeter. My peace. My angels. My kingdom will come to earth in your house. Your children will be blessed there. Your marriage will be blessed there. My Spirit will rest there, and many will sense it. Miracles will happen there. Life will pour from the doors. Do not fear. I have already seen it and it is done. REST in Me, your King. Now, wait and trust and see."

Wow. What a King! How can you doubt after hearing something like that? Well, believe me, you can. How do I know? Because I heard it, and in my inner core I knew it was Him, but I'm still always afraid of putting my own thoughts in when I think I'm hearing Him. I'm afraid of telling myself what I want to hear. And so I don't doubt His goodness, I doubt my own ability to hear.

So while I wanted to believe that Jesus spoke to me, sometimes I'd look at the waves and the fear and the doubt and find myself sinking like Peter did as he was trying to walk on the water towards Jesus. Yet Jesus held out his hand and helped him walk by having him look at Him.

I think there is a great lesson here about faith. If I truly believe that Jesus spoke to me, then I need to listen to what He said. I did believe it, and so after a small battle in my heart, I chose to not listen to the ups and downs that came regarding that house. My emotions couldn't ride those waves anymore. Instead I chose to look straight ahead at Jesus, walk on the water, and let Him pull me to safety.

Then, just like the year before, three days before we were to close on this house the deal fell through completely. The bank had missed one of our sources of income and we actually made too much income to qualify for the loan we had applied for. We didn't qualify for the other loans. It looked like the deal was going to fall through completely. When we heard that news we could have let ourselves sink in despair. Instead we waited calmly for the Lord to intervene because He had said that it was our house. I went to my room and prayed about it in faith. Jesus had said this was our house, so that meant this was just a hiccup.

A few hours later the phone rang. "Mrs. Selvig?" The mortgage employee questioned as I picked up the phone. "I can't believe this, but we found a completely different loan program that I didn't know about. You qualify and not only do you not have to fill out any new paperwork; you'll get an even lower interest rate! We can proceed to closing just as if nothing happened!"

James 1:6 says that he who doubts is like a wave of the sea, driven and tossed by the wind. If I choose to ride every wave I will get beat up by the surf. Choosing to doubt is a choice to be led by emotions and circumstances. If I choose to trust the Word the Lord spoke to me in my prayer time, I can ride through the storm steadily even as waves try to toss me about. Hearing the voice of the Lord is important so that you can face the storms of life with confidence. I can't imagine walking through life without hearing my Shepherd tell me which way to go!

A Personal Story About Hearing God's Voice:

Len and Dagmar Weston are pastors in Piet Retief, South Africa. Here is their story:

"We, a family of five, as theological students & having been in the U.S.A. for eight years, had applied for a green card. It had been denied & with the denial we had been given eight days to leave the US. As can be imagined, our emotions were doing flip-flops, one moment we were trusting God, the next there'd be turmoil & we'd look at the circumstances & then experience understandable fear.

One night we were driving & I was praying, which went something like this: "Lord, You know our predicament. Lead us back into South Africa in the same dramatic way in which You led us out of the States." And in my fertile imaginative mind I was conjuring up a person who would be waiting at the arrivals gate at the International Airport in Johannesburg who was told by God to look for a family of five.

God's plan was different. Immediately after my prayer I experienced a Voice – or was it a thought? – a Thought-Voice which was accompanied by immense peace. And this Thought-Voice communicated this amazingly encouraging message: "Just as you delight in & look forward to giving your children a surprise present, it is with the same delightful expectation that I am waiting to give you the present of where I am leading you." That was it. Simple, effective, and more importantly, it brought peace. That was enough for me. I no longer needed someone to meet us at the airport, I did not need to know where in South Africa we were going to live, GOD had it in control & that was all I needed to know.

I had no way of knowing that He would lead us to a small town in Mpumalanga, in the northeastern part of the country.

Four months later, in the church we felt God had led us to in the town of Piet Retief, the Lord gently reminded me of what He had told me that night months ago. Again He *spoke* to me as a thought in my brain: "Now do you see? THIS is what I was looking forward to giving you!"

Chapter 8

To Share or Not to Share, That is the Question

Hearing a Word From God About Someone Else

Once you begin feeling confident that the Lord is speaking to you in your personal life, He may share something with you about another person. You may get some insight into that person's life or situation, but then you will have to decide what to do with that information.

One of the biggest mistakes I think we make when learning to hear His voice regarding other people is to assume that we are supposed to share the insight with them. Often this results in us looking foolish or the person being embarrassed. Why would God share something with us if we weren't supposed to reveal it? The answer is simple. It's because you are in a relationship with Him. He is a Father and you are a *son* (or daughter). He wants relationship with you and wants to share things on His heart that you can help with. How can you help and how can this knowledge help you? It connects you to the body and if you pray, you grow in your love towards this hurting person and you can actually help them with your prayers.

I would go as far as to say that unless you have a very clear revelation that you are to speak to the person, and/or you are in direct authority or in relationship with the person, that you should assume that your only role is to keep quiet about the revelation and to pray for them.

In previous chapters I told several stories where the Lord revealed to me something about someone else, but I had no relationship with those people and didn't know what to do with the information. When He revealed to me a dark and grievous sin about a certain man I worked with, I cried out to God, "Why did you show that to me? I don't have a relationship with him or any reason to speak into his life. What purpose is there in you showing me that?"

Had I not asked the Lord that question and had I confronted the man, who knows what would have happened? It wouldn't have made his situation better; it probably would have just ridiculed and embarrassed him more. The Lord spoke to me and said, "I told you so you could pray for my son." He wanted me involved in His body and He wanted me to pray for my brother who was about to face public ridicule when the news broke loose of his actions. He was not asking me to judge or confront him.

Relationship and Authority

God is big on relationships and authority (Romans 13:1, Hebrews 12:17, 1 Peter 2:18-20, 1 Timothy 5:17). If you are not in relationship or in authority over a person, you should think really hard before sharing *a word*. If you are in a relationship with someone that God speaks to you about, because of the relationship, they will listen to you. If you are in authority over a person, they have to listen to you. God will use the position or relationship you are in to speak to that person. I do not believe He would choose someone who is out of relationship or authority to speak unless He has to. God is personal that way. If He speaks to you about a person you are not in authority over, and not in relationship with, you should assume your role is to pray and keep quiet.

If you are a minister in a church service and the Lord gives you a word for someone you don't know, as the *minister* you are in authority in that service and technically you qualify to give someone a word. If you are a deacon or a leader in the church and the Lord gives you a word, you also qualify. These are not Biblical guidelines; they are just common sense guidelines. They will protect you and the person you've heard the word about as you learn to hear God's voice.

There are exceptions to every rule and it is possible that the Lord will use you to speak to someone you don't know. I know of situations where a person has nobody in their life who is capable of hearing God and so God uses someone outside of their circle of friends or influence to speak to them. I am just asking you to use caution and to be extra careful if you think God is asking you to speak to someone with whom you have no relationship or authority. Ask God to confirm it to you in other ways before you speak, just to be safe. He may have just given you a word so that you can pray.

Chapter 9

Avoiding Flakiness!

The Art of Learning How Not to Be Flaky

I wish I didn't have to include this chapter, but so much is at stake. If you don't use wisdom and discernment with the people around you while you are learning to hear His voice, mistakes can be made that can turn people away from God. Until you know that you know what His voice sounds like, I believe it is important to take special caution to practice hearing Him out of sight and knowledge of other people. That may sound harsh, but all it really means is that you shouldn't tell other people what you're hearing until you are sure that you are hearing God.

High Mindedness

The first issue that needs to be addressed is that of high mindedness and thinking of oneself more highly than you should. It is an easy trap to think that you are more spiritual than other people if you can hear the voice of the Lord. That humanly makes sense. If you had a couple where the wife hears the voice of the Lord, spends time praying a lot, sees visions, etc. and then her husband does none of this even though he does love God, which would you say is the more spiritual one? Most would say that the wife is more spiritual.

But with God, everything is spiritual. Everyone is spirit. He delights in his children. His spirit is within both the husband and wife. He is in them both and while it may benefit the wife more to be able to hear His voice better, I do not believe that God looks at her as more spiritual or more important. God is the same. He is always speaking to all of us. We are the receivers. Our antennae either picks Him up or it doesn't, but God doesn't love us more if we pick Him up better. This concept is really important if you are to learn how to *not be flaky*. If you start thinking you are a little better than others, people will pick up on it. People can pick up on even just a tiny hint of high mindedness and most are immediately turned off when they detect it. The enemy will use it to destroy your witness and turn others off to what you have to say. Stay humble.

It is for our benefit that we hear the voice of the Lord. He is speaking and loving and drawing us near all the time. He wants His children to come to Him of course, but we should not fall into the trap of becoming judgmental and thinking that we are better or more deserving than anyone else because we have tuned in our receivers to God more than others.

Sharing an Insight or Word When You Shouldn't

I know I've discussed this in earlier chapters, but it is a big part of not being flaky. When God shares something about a person with you, I believe you should not share it with the person unless you have a good relationship with them or if you are in direct authority above them. This is just plain common sense. If you feel God is telling you otherwise in a situation, ask Him to confirm it in two to three ways because it would be the exception not the norm.

God does speak to people about others but often it is so that you will not judge them. Often it is to give you perspective so that you will love them, pray for and support them. We are a body and He wants us to all be connected and to support each other. He also speaks to us about others so that we can gain His perspective in difficult situations.

Chapter 10

Exercises to Help You Hear God Speak

Exercise #1: Journaling

The first place to start when learning to hear God speak is through journaling. For some, journaling comes easy and for others this is going to be a challenge. Buy yourself a spiral bound notebook or journal, or, open up a word document on your computer and save it as *My Prayer Journal*. Either way will work; just have a place to enter your thoughts and prayers. Journaling helped me gain confidence that I was truly hearing God's voice, and I'm certain it will help you too.

My advice is to decide in your heart that you will not share this journal with anyone (except maybe a loving, forgiving friend or spouse who knows that you are trying to learn to hear God).

Begin by writing out (or typing) a prayer to the Lord. Make a habit of praising and thanking Him for blessings in your life. Be honest and tell God how you feel about Him. Explain where you want your relationship with Him to go. Then bring any needs you have to Him. Tell Him what is on your heart and then take a few moments to rest in His peace. When you are ready, close your eyes and listen to your thoughts. Be ready to write. Imagine Jesus is standing or sitting beside you with an approving smile on His face (He definitely approves of you coming to Him and trying to learn to hear His voice.) Then see if you can imagine what He might say to you. This might feel awkward at first. Allow yourself to feel awkward. Don't rush it. Write a response to yourself *from Jesus* and don't think too hard about what you are writing.

What would Jesus say to you to encourage you? What would Jesus say about the needs you have brought to Him? What does Jesus say about your future? Remember, you're just learning how to hear Him. Allow yourself permission to feel awkward. As you're priming the pump and thinking on these things, He is able to speak into your thoughts. You have to trust that what He promised is true. His sheep hear His voice and they know Him. He has sealed you with the Holy Spirit. The Holy Spirit is within you and can and does speak to you in your thoughts.

Write whatever comes to your mind. Know that it is acceptable if some of what you write is from you and not from God. This is practice. It doesn't have to be perfect and doesn't have to be shared with anyone ever. God is not sitting up on His throne ready to strike you if you get it wrong. Jesus' job is to point us to the Father and to help us by covering our shortcomings. God looks at us through His son Jesus, and all has been made right through Him. Jesus is a loving, encouraging Shepherd who is excited that you are trying to hear His voice.

It will take time for you to develop confidence that you are really hearing God rather than making it all up in your head, so just know that ahead of time. And as you journal every day from *God's perspective to you*, be brave to write things that you aren't sure are from Him. Usually when you go back and read what you have written you'll be amazed to see God's voice really did speak. Over time you'll be able to see that the things you are writing down from Him amazingly are true. You'll have more confidence that He really is speaking to you and you'll feel better about your own ability to hear Him. And then journaling can become a way that you use to personally hear God when you need to.

Exercise #2: Road Trip with God

I am a mother of three young children. My youngest being in the toddler years, I can hardly find the time or presence of mind to get my thoughts on paper. Today, while writing this, I have gotten away to a condo up in Winter Park, Colorado. A friend knew that I needed some time to myself to write and offered me a day in her time share (yes, she's an awesome friend!)

I had about a three-hour drive to get to the condo and so I brought along my 35mm camera, knowing I'd see some beautiful things to photograph. In the car I just started talking to Jesus in faith that He really was right there in the car with me. I heard Him speak to my mind saying, "Remember when your dad used to take you out to photograph nature? That was my idea and my doing! Let's do that together today!" I replied with, "I love it! Let's do it." And then I heard Him say, "You're going to get photos of a meadow, a tree, a furry animal and a bird today." Then I felt a little nervous. I was hearing Him through my thoughts, not audibly. If it wasn't really my Lord, I was not going to see these things on my trip and then I would feel foolish. However, I've heard His voice so many times now that I really am getting better at trusting when I hear Him. I was pretty confident I had heard Him on this and started looking forward to seeing these four things.

As I was driving over a mountain pass, I heard him speak in my heart. "Take the first left you can once you've climbed the pass." As I finished climbing the pass, there was a left turn but it was a little tricky to maneuver and it was a gravel turn off. I hesitated. Was I hearing Him or was I acting crazy? In my hesitation I missed the left turn and I kept on going. I knew that I had missed what God had told me to do. However, this has become an amazing lesson for me in God's grace.

It ends up that He made up for my mistake and we still got the four pictures. I didn't fail because I *missed God* the first time. I still pursued the photos after I missed the first turn and He made up for my shortcomings.

So, I took the second "left turn" and I got out and took some pictures. I did find a tree and a meadow, but those are fairly easy to find in Colorado. Whether I had heard God or not would be proven if I saw a furry animal and a bird. Believe it or not, the whole rest of the drive I didn't see a bird or an animal. I got checked into my condo and started writing. If God had truly spoken about this he was going to have to bring the bird and the furry animal to me.

I wrote and I prayed and after about four or five hours of working I heard a noise outside my condo door. It sounded like a child was crying. I ignored it assuming it was a neighbor's child, but a few minutes later, I heard it again. I peeked out the window and there was a furry fox sitting there looking at me. God had brought the furry animal to me! He was sitting on the ledge just waiting for me to take his photo. I took my camera and got my shot. Jesus truly brought this fox so that I could share with you that I had heard His voice.

The fox that came to me for a photo.

Wendy Selvig

The tree, the bird and the meadow that the Lord had told me I would find on the journey.

A few moments after the fox came, my favorite Colorado bird, the Magpie, came swooping down and landed about 10 feet in front of me and pranced around on the lawn in front of me. He literally paced back and forth as if waiting for me to take the picture. I snapped the photo and he took off. Between the fox and the bird coming to me for their photos to be taken, I was feeling a bit like Snow White!

The first two photos I got during my drive. I honestly could have gotten those without the Lord's help. The tree and the meadow were things that were typical. The second two He had to bring to me. The bird wasn't just a bird in a tree that I happened to get. The bird came to me. He looked like he was deliberately prancing in front of my condo…and the fox, well just look at the picture and tell me if God did or didn't bring him directly for a great picture.

God cares about your everyday life. If He can speak to me in this manner, He can and will speak to you. I'm here to cheer you on and encourage you to try to hear Him. It takes faith. It takes practice. I feel like every time I hear Him it is practice. I don't ever feel like I've quite figured it out.

I encourage you to realize that Jesus wants you to practice hearing His voice. He wants you to try to hear Him. Try the following exercises and don't beat yourself up if you don't get it the first time. He will help and honor you if you just try. Practice and listen and don't feel like you have to tell people what you're up to. You don't need other people criticizing you while you're learning to hear God's voice. Keep it between you and God because it's all about developing the intimacy and trust between you and Jesus anyway.

Here's how you can take a photo journey with God too. You don't have to be a photographer, even a point and shoot camera will work. This is about hearing Him not about taking photo competition worthy photos.

Take your camera and go on a journey with the Lord. Take your journal. Pray first and ask Jesus to be with you as you travel and to speak to you to help you learn how to hear His voice. Ask Him to tell you three or four things that you are going to see on your journey and get a picture of. Get really quiet and write down the things that come to mind. Have faith that He is in you, He has sealed you with His Spirit and that you really can hear Him speaking through your thoughts. Pray and ask Him where you should go. Do any locations pop into your mind? Do you feel peace or unrest as you think more about these locations? Pick the location that you feel the most peaceful about and head that way. As you practice and get better at this, you will be able to hear thoughts from Him like, "Turn left the next time you can," without feeling foolish. I know this sounds crazy to some, but He really is that personable and He really is with you if you want Him to be. Keep your journal with you and pause to write throughout the trip. It will be exciting to read after you are finished!

Exercise #3: Garage Sales With God

This is a great exercise that you can do without telling anyone you are doing it. It gives you a great opportunity to sort out the impressions you are getting in your heart. Once you get confident of God's voice, this is a great exercise to do with your kids as well to show them He really does speak. Pick something you need or are looking for at a garage sale and then pray about it. Ask God to reveal to you where you might find the item and imagine a map of the city in your head. See if your thoughts gravitate to any specific area on the map. Does one area pop out more than others? Imagine looking around the map at all the different parts of town. Does anything stick out more than another? Do you have any thoughts or pictures of any specific intersections or neighborhoods come up in your head? If so, go with it. Drive to that neighborhood (on a Friday or Saturday morning in the summer when there are garage sales) and drive around looking for sales. God might just lead you to the house you need to go to find the item you prayed about! The first time I did this exercise, I needed to find an umbrella stroller and a regular stroller. I told my then six-year-old that we were going to pray and ask God to show us where to go to get the strollers. We prayed together and then when I started thinking of all the neighborhoods, one in particular seemed to rise above the others in my mind. I immediately drove to that neighborhood and there was a big garage sale that we found. As soon as we pulled up I saw two strollers sitting on the curb, both were the kinds I was looking for! I praised God for helping me hear and for helping me to let my child in on the learning experience!

These exercises are designed to help you press through to victory in hearing the voice of Jesus in your life.

We cannot see the heavenly realm, but there are many clues that tell us it is here. It takes faith to believe you can hear the voice of God, but if you believe in the spirit realm and you belong to the Lord and are sealed with his Holy Spirit, don't you think you should be able to hear Him? Just knowing it is possible is half the battle. Practicing is the other half. The Lord wants you to hone this skill. He is going to help you along the way. He is not condemning you for trying and failing. If you ever feel like God is telling you to do something that makes you uneasy, don't do it. Blame it on me if you like, but be willing to fail a test before you listen and act on the wrong voice. Do the lesson over and over to make sure you're hearing God's voice.

I had someone once tell me about trying to learn to hear God's voice and they were driving and randomly would have a thought to suddenly turn here or there and there was no peace in it, only anxiety. I would say that you ignore thoughts like this. Resist them. The enemy will eventually flee when he sees you resisting. Jesus leads with peace, and He is a very smart and patient King. He is not giving you a score on these lessons; you do not have to worry about failing. He patiently will be with you until you get it right. Don't listen to any fear or panic or anxiety.

For example, on my photo journey I had heard the Lord say to take the first left turn over the mountain pass. Well as I went over the pass there was an immediate turn off that I was uncertain about because it wasn't a road, just a pull over. It caused a little anxiety because the Lord had said to me, 'Take the first turnoff' over the pass. There were cars behind me and I wasn't going to cause an accident so I was willing to miss God on that and keep going. If I sensed Him later telling me to go back, I would have. Instead, there was a definite turn off a little later down the road that looked better and I took that. I prayed about it and had the sense that even if the other turnoff had been the one God had originally intended, He would still make this one work. He would rise to meet me since I was still trying to hear. This was an exercise, not a life or death situation. Hey, at least I turned off! It's possible that I would have seen a bird, a furry animal, a tree and a meadow all at that first turn off. Instead, I took the second turnoff and saw a tree and meadow…and later God brought the animal and the bird to me at my condo. He helped me along the journey and made up for my inability to hear or know if indeed I was supposed to take that first turnoff.

Remember, He is the *Prince of Peace* and He will work with you. Don't ever be led by fear or anxiety. If you're anxious about what you are hearing, declare the test over, go home and journal about it. Pray about it and see what conclusions you come to about the voice you were listening to.

Always write it down. Ask Him to speak, listen quietly, and write down the *impression* you get in your mind and emotions. Be willing to be wrong. Don't share it with anyone. Be willing to develop this skill over time. Wait and let Him bring the answer to you. Make sure you journal the answer if you were right or wrong. If you were wrong, make a note of which voice you heard instead of God's. Did it belong to the enemy or was it your own? Pray, thank God for exercises and try again. You are on a fabulous journey that only leads to you coming closer to Jesus.

There are all sorts of variations on the photo journey that you could take. Pick something you like to do. Do you like to go to basketball games? Ask the Lord to share with you three things you will see or experience at the game and then write down the impressions you get. If you fail and somehow don't see them, it is not a big deal. Try again with another thing. Maybe you like to hike? Ask the Lord to tell you three things you might see that are odd on a hike. You can do the same thing with anything you like to do - a movie, a concert, a drive. All are activities that you can do with the Lord and in journaling and asking Him to speak to you; you can practice to hear His voice.

Chapter 11

Teaching Your Children To Hear God Speak

Being Intentional With Our Kids

It's easy to be so distracted with adult life that we forget to be intentional with our kids. I often find myself coasting in certain areas, and then I see my lack of intentionality show up in my children's behavior later. Unfortunately, being intentional requires an upfront investment, so if I want to see results in certain areas, I have to make the effort.

Before you start to feel overwhelmed or judged, please know I'm as guilty as the next parent in forgetting to be intentional. I don't think anyone can be perfect about being intentional in every area, but if we pick a few important areas to remain consistent in, we'll start to see good results over time.

For me, teaching my kids how to hear the voice of the Lord is an important goal. Think about what it would look like if your kids were confident that the Holy Spirit lived within them, that He spoke to and guided them, and they listened to His voice and sought Him before they made decisions. Wow, parenting just got a whole lot easier!

I want my kids to know who they are, to know the big picture in life, and to know that Jesus walks with them through the valleys and the mountain top experiences. I want them to know the confidence and safety that comes with trusting their Father in Heaven with their lives.

Children can accept the Lord Jesus as their Savior from very young ages. Many come to Christ with their childlike faith at three or four years of age. If they can choose to believe in Him, they also can learn to hear His voice in their lives. We can help our children hear His voice and we can help cultivate the desire to obey the voice of the Lord within their own hearts. While I don't want parents to feel pressure that their little ones have to be hearing God's voice, I think that if we intentionally teach our kids to recognize that the Holy Spirit is within them and that He is speaking, He who began a good work in them will carry it on to completion (Phil. 1:6)!

As parents, we all come from different walks of life. We all grew up differently. Some people had wonderful Godly parents who raised them knowing the Lord, while others had no Christian influence in their childhood at all. As parents, how do we raise our children to know Him?

I don't feel like I own the corner on this, but I can offer what has seemed to work for our family. I think it starts with introducing our kids to Jesus as a real person that we cannot physically see with our eyes. Explaining to them that Jesus is at the right hand of the Father (why we can't see Him right now) and He is there praying for us and helping us. It's important that they know He can hear our prayers. The Holy Spirit who lives in us is directly connected to Jesus. He hears it when we reach out to Him.

Leading By Example

The best way to help solidify this thought is for them to see you praying and talking to Jesus. Praying with them at bedtime, at dinner and whenever there is a need is a good start. They need to see that we as adults come to Jesus too.

The goal is for them to eventually start trusting Him for their own needs, or they will never make the crossover. It will always be *mom and dad's religion* if they never learn to trust God for their own struggles and walk in life. They need to see and know that God is real. When they start to see God answer their own prayers, He will become real to them. The childhood years are the opportune time to help them practice trusting in God.

Encourage Them To Write

With my own kids, I saw incredible spiritual growth in them when they were old enough to write. I make sure they have journals and encourage them to write in them. Even when my son Caleb was seven, I would encourage him to draw pictures about God. He started writing that year and again I saw growth when he could write his thoughts out to God.

I am not perfect in this endeavor. I'm not as consistent as I wish I were, but I do encourage them to write their prayers to God at night and other opportune times.

Recently my kids were home from school because of a snow day. They wanted to play video games and I didn't mind them playing for a while, but before they were allowed to play, I had them go to their rooms for 15 minutes to have some quiet time and write out some prayers to God.

My 11-year-old came to me and told me that he felt God had told him he was part of something big but that he just couldn't see what it is yet. He had written in it his journal and dated it, just like I've shown him how to do.

I can't tell you what a joy to my heart it was to see that he was journaling and hearing the Spirit of God in his thoughts.

My seven-year-old told me that he didn't really hear anything (and I told him it was fine!) but he showed me his paper and my heart burst seeing what he wrote (in his own writing).

"Dear God, I love you varee much. I cooold reward you with varee much stuff but I don't have anuf (to give) so I wunt to let you to know my love instead of stuf."

His heart is being cultivated and the Holy Spirit is working in it because he is speaking the language of love. God is love. His Spirit is within my son and I can see the fruit of the Spirit in his words.

Kids can get this! Kids can learn to trust God and know Him!

Wendy Selvig

Teenagers Need To See God Answering Prayers

I worry about teenagers in the United States. Teens are confronted with the evils of the world every day but often do not find hope from the Church or loved ones that God is strong enough or powerful enough to help them overcome.

I don't' want to be a downer on the Church in the United States but I feel that so much of basic faith has been watered down in many places. Many denominations deny the power of God and don't challenge people to have faith. If this sounds like your church, for the sake of your teen, run (don't walk) away and find a life-giving church where you see people loving each other and exercising their faith. Ask God to lead you to a place where you can get infused with life-giving teachings and where you can grow in faith.

For me as a teenager, my walk with God was solidified when I saw Him answering prayers. When I saw His hand at work, I realized that He was real. I was asking the tough questions that most teenagers ask. Was God real? Was He good? Was Satan real? Was he powerful or not?

My older brother was a pastor during my teen years. At his church I saw a man healed when the pastors all prayed for him. His leg was shorter than the other and I watched it grow several inches as they prayed. I then had faith to pray for myself when I was diagnosed with an incurable skin disease. I laid hands on my teenage self and said, "In the name of Jesus I command you to leave my body." Instantly the pain and itching stopped and within 24 hours all the lesions were dried up. *That* answered a few of my tough questions and solidified my faith. I got answers to questions from the One that mattered. I saw that He was alive and though the answer wasn't always the one I hoped for, I did see answers and I saw that He was good.

Teens ask tough questions because they are trying to figure out who they are and what they believe. I've found that most teens are incredibly loyal and passionate about God when they realize that He is real, He is good, and He has authority over evil.

They do have to understand the big picture and that we live in a broken world that is waiting for a time when Christ comes back and redeems it. Sometimes evil overcomes good in the battle on this earth. But, when they understand that this life is temporary, is a test of sorts, and that Jesus promises to walk through life with us – whether valley, plain or mountain top, they are encouraged. And, when they learn to hear His voice and recognize they are not alone, it can make all the difference.

So what kind of questions are they asking? Here's a few I dealt with as a teenager: If Satan is alive and well, is he more powerful than God? Is it easier to believe there is no God and no Satan and that we are all just a product of our circumstances? That one seems easier to stomach than Satan being more powerful, or even worse, God being more powerful but choosing not to help us in our need.

Teenagers are thinking about these things and your teens will too. We must show them how real and alive He is through intentional parenting in this area.

Yes, family devotions can be meaningful. Yes, church and Sunday school can help shape their minds. You can tell them what you believe until you are blue in the face, but until they are challenged to trust God on their own-- it will never be their own faith. They are not going to pick up faith through osmosis! Just going to Sunday school and being around Christians is not going to convince them of anything. This may require a few heart to heart discussions, giving them a book like this one, and a challenge to not miss the big picture of life. And of course, they need your prayers.

To raise children who are unwavering in their faith, you have to intentionally introduce them to the person of Jesus and teach and guide them how to pray and how to listen to His voice. They have to know that He is speaking to them personally and that He is there to walk with them through every trial. They should be encouraged to pray for things with their childlike faith and when they see prayers answered, it solidifies in their heart that what they are learning is real. Help them to experience Christ at a young age so that they will not part from Him later.

Steps You Can Take To Help Your Kids Trust God

1. **Don't underestimate the power of prayer**. Specifically ask God to open their ears to hear His voice. Pray for your children that they will hear God's voice at an early age. Pray that they will have the wisdom of God and understanding of who God is and that

the god of this age (Satan) will not be able to blind their eyes to God and His Kingdom.

2. **Have childlike faith with them**. Kids have faith naturally. When they want to believe God for something, be willing to have faith with them. If they want to lay hands on a sick pet, be willing to pray with them.

    If they pray for the family pet and then he/she doesn't get well, it is a good opportunity to explain how the world we live in is a broken world. You can explain that one day everything will be restored (Acts 3:21) and made whole again, but until then both good and bad things happen. We have to trust God that He is good and that He doesn't desire evil for us. His Word says that He knows the plans He has for us, plans for a hope and a future (Jeremiah 29:11). Any evil in our lives comes from the fact that we have an enemy and that we live in the middle of a battleground. Casualties and losses happen but it is not because God willed it. He is allowing us to live in an age (for a period of time) where life is what it is and we live in a battle. It requires faith in His goodness and the ability to hear His voice so that He can steer us from trouble.

    And, God promises to be close to the broken hearted, so He sees your children's hearts and their pain and is with them. Encourage them to tell God how they feel and to trust Him to take care of their sick pet until they get to see him/her again in heaven.

3. **Don't seed doubt**. My first two sons, have each had an experience where they came out of their rooms saying, "what mom?" I answered, "I didn't say anything." They both clearly thought they heard me calling them. I told them, "Maybe that was God calling your name." I remembered that in 1 Samuel 3, the Lord spoke to Samuel as a child too and he did not know it was God. I don't know if it was the Lord or not, but I wasn't going to be the one to seed doubt into their minds that it was nothing. I understand that the Holy Spirit speaks to us through our thoughts. He may have been calling out to my sons.

4. **Have important conversations with them**. Timing is important when having conversations about God. When they are watching

TV or playing a game, the timing is not right to strike up a conversation. My advice is to wait until they are bored or are doing something they'd rather not be doing (like going to bed). You will have more of their attention if they are getting out of bedtime by listening to you. I love talking about God right before bedtime so that their little minds can simmer on it all night long, even in their sleep.

Use travel time in the car when they are young to have important conversations about God. When my oldest sons were nine and six they responded well to this question: "If someone said to you that God spoke to them, how do you think they heard Him? Do you think they heard His voice just like you hear me talking? Do you think it was like a thought in their head? What do you think?" My nine year old responded with, "Hmmm, that is a good question! I don't know." My six year old piped up with, "I think they would hear Him like you are speaking now." Then, I was able to discuss how God can speak both ways, but because the Holy Spirit is in us, He often speaks to our minds through thoughts.

5. **When you see God work in the details of your life, share it with your kids**. Every time I see God show up in my day, I tell my kids about it. I want them to get used to recognizing His hand in regular life. Today, as I'm writing this, the Lord miraculously provided over a thousand dollars for a bill that was due. The exact amount we needed came in from an unexpected and unsolicited source on the same day we needed to pay it. I told the kids all about it and they smiled and could see how miraculous that really was. They saw God work in mom and dad's life, so it will be easier for them to trust Him to work in theirs when they are ready.

Intentional Topics for Discussion with Your Kids

These may help cultivate your kids' ability to recognize the voice of God in their lives:

Fruit of the Spirit: Discuss the fruit of the Holy Spirit. Have the fruits written down ahead of time and ask them what they think each one of the fruits mean. This could be broken into many conversations as you ponder each one. What is love? What does it mean to really love someone? Who do you love? Do you love the person who is mean to you? Should you love that person? What does it look like to love that person? How does God see that person, does He love them? (Joy, Peace, Patience, Kindness, Self-Control) The fruits of the Spirit are in essence, attributes of God. God is love. He is the Prince of Peace. He is Kind. When we are listening to thoughts in our head and trying to figure out where they come from, if they have the fruit of the Spirit, they are probably from God! Satan is our enemy and he has some bad guys working with him. If your enemy could give you thoughts what would he say? It wouldn't sound like the fruit of the Spirit that is for sure. What kind of thoughts are the opposite of God's thoughts? Have them answer but you can be ready with some examples such as thoughts that are mean, hateful, judgmental, rebellious, and rude, causing harm not good.

Teach them to tune out the noise: Explain that sometimes it is hard to hear God's voice because there is so much noise around us these days. The TV, radio, iPods, video games, and computers all make noise and attract our attention. It's hard to think about God when we get so distracted by other fun entertaining things.

Here's one great intentional exercise you can do in the car with your kids. Ask one of your children to say the ABC's to another child. Turn up the radio (with a smile on your face, don't be mean about it) when he starts to speak. Then turn the radio down and ask the other child if it was difficult to hear his/her sibling when the radio was up. In the same way, when our attention is grabbed by all these other fun things, we can't hear God speaking very well either.

Learning to be quiet: Encourage them to have time (even one minute) where they sit still and quiet and pray and listen for God's thoughts. If they are old enough to write, encourage them to have a quiet time where they pray and then write down what they think God may be saying.

Eternity: Discuss what eternity means. How long is eternity? Draw a line on a piece of paper with arrows at each end, showing that the line goes off the paper. Then, mark about an inch of the line and show them that the inch represents 100 years of life for a human. Discuss how God gives us the time that we have on the earth to go through a test. The test is all about when life is tough; whose side are we going to be on. Will we learn to love and trust God? Will we learn to help others? Or, will we decide to be selfish and live for ourselves only? Whatever we do in that short period of time determines our home and position for eternity. This is a heavy topic but important so that our children begin to think about what is beyond our life here. They like to think about it. Be prepared for all kinds of questions about heaven!

Faith: What is faith? Is having faith something that pleases God? Why does God want us to have faith? How do we have faith when times are hard?

Emotions: Do you ever feel like you can sense God being with you? If you don't feel that, does it mean He isn't with you? Have a discussion about feelings and how it is nice when you sense God and feel Him, but that He promises to always be with us. If we don't feel Him, it's just that our "feelers" aren't working. We can trust Him to always be there for us.

Prayer Journal: When your kids are old enough, buy them a prayer journal and encourage them to write their prayers to God. Then, explain the idea of writing responses from God in their journal. Kids usually get this much better than adults. If you can teach them to hear God speaking at a young age, you'll give them an invaluable tool!

Prayer Rock Jar: It's important to remember the answers to prayers. Once a prayer is answered it is easy to move on to the next prayer request and forget earlier answered prayers.

One way to help your family remember answered prayers is to have an answered prayer rock jar. Every time you have an answer to prayer, you put a rock in the jar and you write down the answer in a book. Then at the end of the year, or Thanksgiving or even several years down the road, your kids look at that jar and see a visual representation of every answered prayer. It builds their faith and probably will build yours too! You just have to stay diligent at filling that jar!

Another option is to buy a journal that is specifically for prayers and answered prayers. As your family shares prayer requests, write them down in the journal. Pray as a family over the requests and then periodically review the requests and write in the margin how God answered. Have faith. He answers! That prayer journal could become a treasured family heirloom!

These are just ideas to help you get started being intentional with your kids. The best way they will learn to trust in God is to see you actively trusting Him. I encourage you to share with your kids some of your own prayer requests and then by all means, share when He answers them.

As you learn to hear God and they see Him speak to you, it will encourage them to hear God for themselves as well. The main point is to get them thinking about hearing God at an early age. If they know God speaks through thoughts and not in some audible booming voice, they will be more aware as they grow up that He may be speaking to them!

Chapter 12

A Higher Conscience

I have heard it suggested that people don't hear God's voice but that instead, their higher evolutionary self has tapped into the common consciousness of humanity.

I have to fight to maintain my graciousness on this argument. Secularists in our culture present that we are who we are because we have evolved there on our own. The argument would be that people who think they hear God have developed some way to access an inner communal wisdom (like an ant), answering our own thoughts as if that voice were God. (And really, if you believe this, why is it so difficult to take it one step further and believe that the inner wisdom comes from some One rather than coming from evolved brain matter?)

It's an empowering idea to believe that we've tapped into some collective consciousness or some power of the communal brain. To me it's bunk. It sounds like parapsychological Hollywood ideologies that sound nice but aren't true. How do I know? Because the One who speaks to us does more than speak, He gets involved. He backs His words up. He supports His words with actions and proves Himself to anyone willing to see.

The One who speaks is not an *inner consciousness* and is not my own intellect answering my own questions. I do not have a split personality and the *God* voice I am hearing is not the *good me* versus the *bad me*.

He is God. He is *the One*. He is the One who made us and is calling to us. He desires to have a relationship with us. He is bigger than any box we can dream up for Him, and He speaks if we are willing to listen.

And then, God does more than speak. He acts. External circumstances change when He gets involved. He is a shepherd. The Bible says He is the *Good Shepherd* and He walks beside us.

Psalms 23 says I shall not be in want. He makes me lie down in green pastures, He leads me beside quiet waters, and He restores my soul. He guides me in paths of righteousness for His name's sake. His rod and staff comfort me.

This is a picture of the Lord walking beside someone who has asked Him to be the Lord of their lives. He is invisible, but His Spirit is very real and He promises to walk with us and lead and guide us even through the valley of the shadow of death (Ps. 23:4). He is always with you. He is there to be your counselor when you need one. He promises not to leave or forsake you. He is always there gently leading.

One summer in college I spent two months in Uganda, Africa. I was on a mission team with other college students and we went throughout the country holding meetings where we would preach God's Word and then pray and minister to the people. We all took turns speaking and I was pretty nervous the first time I had to do it. We were in an open outside area of a village and the village people all came out and stood around while we preached God's Word, and someone interpreted what we said. I preached the message I felt God had prepared me with. The whole time I was preaching, there was a young African man standing towards the back of the crowd.

Though I don't remember God speaking specifically to me about him, I felt the Lord was asking me to notice him. My eyes were drawn to him as I was preaching. He was intensely listening to what I was saying. I could see the intensity etched into his face.

After the service was over, we were praying for people and he came forward and asked me to pray. His name was Thomas. He believed in Jesus and wanted to ask Him to be his Lord, but was so torn because his family was all of another religion and he could be cast out of his family and community if he accepted Jesus. He had been visiting this village and was to leave in the next day or two to go back to his college and we would probably never see him again. But the Lord burned the image of this young man into my mind and gave me some words of peace to speak to him. I don't remember the exact words, but I told him something along the lines that if he asked Jesus into his heart and trusted God, God would work on his family. He prayed with me, asked the Lord Jesus to come into his life and to start leading him, and later we said our goodbyes. I never thought I'd see him again.

We left that village and continued to travel. We went from village to village and town to town. We literally traveled all over Uganda. Sometimes we would stop in bigger towns and cities and preach at churches. Other times we'd find ourselves teaching in little country huts out in the middle of a field.

Several weeks after meeting Thomas we were in a bigger town where there was a hospital. We went into the hospital to visit and pray for those who were sick. There was one man who we prayed for who had Yellow Fever. I don't know if you know anything about Yellow Fever but it is a miserable disease. The Lord told me to go and lay hands on this man with the Yellow Fever. He spoke Lugandan and not English and so his daughter who was by his bedside interpreted for us. After asking if I could pray for him, and them agreeing to the idea, I laid my hand on his arm. He was lying in a hospital bed and was so weak he could not sit up. I just lightly touched him and began to pray. As I prayed I felt my arm start to heat up. Before long I felt an increasing heat in my arm and I knew that heat was the power of God within me, flowing to this man to heal him from the disease. I was excited and kept praying. The daughter began to get excited as she was translating what the father was saying. The father was saying, "it's hot, it's hot! Heat is coming from your hands!" When I felt a release in my heart, it was as if the Lord had said to me, "It is finished." I stopped praying. The man's eyes were as wide as saucers. He had experienced something. He began speaking wildly and his daughter interpreted. He said that he had felt the power of God and that he wanted to know how to know this *Jesus* I had prayed in the name of. He wanted to know how to make him the God of his life. We of course explained and prayed with him and his daughter, who both received the Lord that day as their new Shepherd.

Later in the same hospital, while still praying for people, I remember walking down a corridor. As I went around the corner I almost literally ran into someone. When I looked up, I could not believe my eyes. It was Thomas, the young man we had reached out to in a village several weeks before. His eyes grew large and he began speaking quickly and loudly. "Praise to God, He has answered my prayers! Praise to God, He has answered my prayers!" When I got him to calm down he explained to me, "I trusted Jesus to be my Lord and asked Him to save my family. My father is in this hospital and my whole family is here with him. He is very ill. I told them about Jesus and they told me that they would consider Jesus if they could hear the same preaching that I heard. We make decisions as a family and the whole family wants to hear together about Jesus. I asked God to send you back to us somehow, even though I didn't know what town you were in or how to find you, to tell my family about God and now you are here! Praise to God he has answered my prayers!"

God had miraculously brought us to the very town his father was in, and He had brought us to the very hospital Thomas's father was in. I stepped into the tiny hospital room, feeling very bold at that moment in faith and excitement with what God was doing. I explained to his family about how God's simple gift to them was salvation and eternal life and all they had to do was accept the gift and begin trusting God to walk with them through life. They discussed what I told them and then as a family they all knelt down in the hospital room and gave their lives to Jesus.

Our team left the hospital that day very encouraged. This is a journey on our part as well. It takes faith to tell someone that God will "work it out" with his family. And that faith is more than just hoping God will work it out. It is knowing God by reading the Word and getting it down inside you so that you know what God's response is to situations and knowing what the Word says He will do. Then when circumstances come up that challenge your faith, you know you can tell someone what the Bible says that God will do, and it is true every time. He really keeps His Word. John 1:1 says that Jesus is the Word of God in flesh form. The Word of God is a manual to know who Jesus is. He can't depart from it, it is Him.

By the way, on our way out of the hospital that day, I stopped by the room of the man who had had Yellow Fever. Before he was healed he had been lying in bed without the energy to sit up. As we stopped to say goodbye, he was sitting straight up, was full of energy and was smiling ear to ear. He had been completely healed and was waiting for a doctor to come confirm it. He was so happy and thankful and excited to start his life with this new Savior who cared enough to touch him in a physical way. My inner consciousness did not heal the man; my Savior Jesus Christ healed him. My inner consciousness did not lead me to Thomas, Jesus Christ led me to him in answer to his prayers. God got involved in the external circumstance which shows His voice is more than communal wisdom.

A Little Word About Faith

Faith is not blind trust in something that you'll never see results from, it is trusting that what God says about Himself in His Word is true, and that you can count on Him to do what He says. Faith can start as small as a mustard seed and grows as you see Him lead and guide in your life. Faith is the currency of a supernatural kingdom you may have never even known was there. Don't feel like you have to move mountains with your faith at the beginning, it's OK to start with just a tiny bit. It's hard to describe what real faith looks like, because it is not just hope. There is more to it than *hoping* He'll come through.

Matthew 9:29 says that 'according to your faith it will be done to you.' It does not say, 'according to your hope.' The substance of faith is trusting and believing. Hebrews 11 says that faith is being sure of what we hope for, and certain of what we do not see. Faith is more than hope, its being certain that God will be true to His word, and that if you are asking for something that lines up with His Word, and you believe Him and do not doubt, that He will certainly do it. Faith can be hard to come by when you do not know His Word and His promises. Therefore to hear His voice and to have faith, you must read the Bible and get His Word down into your very being. So to hear the voice of God, you must absolutely start with reading the Bible and getting to know the ideas and concepts and words of Christ that are in it.

Chapter 13

Conclusion

I hope you've enjoyed this book and truly I hope you are able to hear His voice better because of it! When the Lord put it on my heart to write on this topic, I struggled with a lot of self-doubt in my own ability to write and so I put it off for years. It was only in obedience to the urgent sense I felt from the Lord to write it, that I got it finished. My prayer is that you are able to understand the ideas well enough and that your walk with the Lord is strengthened because of this book.

My friend, (and that's what you are if you've read this far) be encouraged. Life is a gift. It's difficult, no doubt. You've assuredly been through difficulties that I have not, and I have been through things you have not, but He has been there with us through all of it. You never have to be alone. You will only be alone if you choose to alienate yourself from the One who made and loves you. And even then, He never leaves you. God is intimately connected with us and loves us so much. Jesus is a real person with a real personality and you can get to know Him through His Word, prayer and learning to hear His voice. He wants to be involved in every part of our lives. The Bible tells us to "pray without ceasing." The Holy Spirit is not offended when we ask Him to help us find our car keys, but hopefully that is not the only time we include Him in our lives. With practice, we can be confident of His voice and we can live a Holy Spirit led life without appearing flaky to others.

I find that my life changed when the big picture of life started to become real to me. When I started seeing that this life is going to be judged and that someone is keeping track of what goes on in my life. I want to win the race. I want to finish well. So, the basic concepts I hold on to are as follows:

1. We don't see the big picture clearly. There is truly more things going on in this life than meet the eye and to be successful I need to trust the One who sees it all.

2. Life is more or less a test. There is judgment at the end, which makes it a test to me. There will be a day where I will have wished I had more foresight to work towards the goal of passing that test and coming out strong on that day.

3. Hearing the voice of God is something we were designed to do and we need to be able to do it to live life well. Voices are speaking to us all the time. We don't have a choice to *opt out* and not listen to any voices. Our minds pick up voices from demons, our fallen nature and who knows what else, and then they interpret the voices as thoughts. We have to know how to rightly discern thoughts and dismiss them if they are not from God.

There is a difference between making it through life as one escaping through the fire (1 Corinthians 3:15), and walking through life victoriously as one who wins a prize and gains a crown (1 Corinthians 9:24-25). Both options are offered to you in this life. If you learn to hear the voice of the One who created the human race and who understands the pitfalls, you will surely be on track to win a crown.

I hope you have the tools you need now to walk more confidently in hearing the Lord and that you indeed will find yourself Snatchproof.

Thank you for reading this book. If you have a story you would like to share about how God has spoken to you, you can contact the author at: WendySelvig@gmail.com You can also find more resources at Snatchproof.org.

CPSIA information can be obtained at www.ICGtesting.com
Printed in the USA
LVOW07s0223071214

417549LV00005B/15/P